Research And Development Tax Credit Complete Self-Assessment Guide

CW01095970

The guidance in this Self-Assessment is based on Research And Development Tax Credit best practices and standards in business process architecture, design and quality management. The guidance is also based on the professional judgment of the individual collaborators listed in the Acknowledgments.

Notice of rights

Trademarks

Table of Contents

About The Art of Service

The Art of Service, Business Process Architects since 2000, is dedicated to helping stakeholders achieve excellence.

Defining, designing, creating, and implementing a process to solve a stakeholders challenge or meet an objective is the most valuable role… In EVERY group, company, organization and department.

Unless you're talking a one-time, single-use project, there should be a process. Whether that process is managed and implemented by humans, AI, or a combination of the two, it needs to be designed by someone with a complex enough perspective to ask the right questions.

Someone capable of asking the right questions and step back and say, 'What are we really trying to accomplish here? And is there a different way to look at it?'

With The Art of Service's Standard Requirements Self-Assessments, we empower people who can do just that — whether their title is marketer, entrepreneur, manager, salesperson, consultant, Business Process Manager, executive assistant, IT Manager, CIO etc... —they are the people who rule the future. They are people who watch the process as it happens, and ask the right questions to make the process work better.

Contact us when you need any support with this Self-Assessment and any help with templates, blue-prints and examples of standard documents you might need:

http://theartofservice.com
service@theartofservice.com

Included Resources - how to access

Included with your purchase of the book is the Research

And Development Tax Credit Self-Assessment Spreadsheet Dashboard which contains all questions and Self-Assessment areas and auto-generates insights, graphs, and project RACI planning - all with examples to get you started right away.

How? Simply send an email to
access@theartofservice.com
with this books' title in the subject to get the Research And Development Tax Credit Self Assessment Tool right away.

You will receive the following contents with New and Updated specific criteria:

- The latest quick edition of the book in PDF

- The latest complete edition of the book in PDF, which criteria correspond to the criteria in...

- The Self-Assessment Excel Dashboard, and...

- Example pre-filled Self-Assessment Excel Dashboard to get familiar with results generation

- In-depth specific Checklists covering the topic

- Project management checklists and templates to assist with implementation

INCLUDES LIFETIME SELF ASSESSMENT UPDATES

Every self assessment comes with Lifetime Updates and Lifetime Free Updated Books. Lifetime Updates is an industry-first feature which allows you to receive verified self assessment updates, ensuring you always have the most accurate information at your fingertips.

Get it now- you will be glad you did - do it now, before you forget.

Send an email to **access@theartofservice.com** with this books' title in the subject to get the Research And Development Tax Credit Self Assessment Tool right away.

Purpose of this Self-Assessment

This Self-Assessment has been developed to improve understanding of the requirements and elements of Research And Development Tax Credit, based on best practices and standards in business process architecture, design and quality management.

It is designed to allow for a rapid Self-Assessment to determine how closely existing management practices and procedures correspond to the elements of the Self-Assessment.

The criteria of requirements and elements of Research And Development Tax Credit have been rephrased in the format of a Self-Assessment questionnaire, with a seven-criterion scoring system, as explained in this document.

In this format, even with limited background knowledge of Research And Development Tax Credit, a manager can quickly review existing operations to determine how they measure up to the standards. This in turn can serve as the starting point of a 'gap analysis' to identify management tools or system elements that might usefully be implemented in the organization to help improve overall performance.

How to use the Self-Assessment

On the following pages are a series of questions to identify to what extent your Research And Development Tax Credit initiative is complete in comparison to the requirements set in standards.

To facilitate answering the questions, there is a space in front of each question to enter a score on a scale of '1' to '5'.

1 Strongly Disagree

2 Disagree

3 Neutral

4 Agree

5 Strongly Agree

Read the question and rate it with the following in front of mind:

'In my belief,
the answer to this question is clearly defined'.

There are two ways in which you can choose to interpret this statement;
1. how aware are you that the answer to the question is clearly defined
2. for more in-depth analysis you can choose to gather evidence and confirm the answer to the question. This obviously will take more time, most Self-Assessment users opt for the first way to interpret the question and dig deeper later on based on the outcome of the overall Self-Assessment.

A score of '1' would mean that the answer is not clear at all, where a '5' would mean the answer is crystal clear and defined. Leave emtpy when the question is not applicable or you don't want to answer it, you can skip it without affecting your score. Write your score in the space provided.

After you have responded to all the appropriate statements in each section, compute your average score for that section, using the formula provided, and round to the nearest tenth. Then transfer to the corresponding spoke in the Research And Development Tax Credit Scorecard on the second next page of the Self-Assessment.

Your completed Research And Development Tax Credit Scorecard will give you a clear presentation of which Research And Development Tax Credit areas need attention.

Research And Development Tax Credit Scorecard Example

Example of how the finalized Scorecard can look like:

Research And Development Tax Credit Scorecard

Your Scores:

BEGINNING OF THE SELF-ASSESSMENT:

CRITERION #1: RECOGNIZE

INTENT: Be aware of the need for change. Recognize that there is an unfavorable variation, problem or symptom.

In my belief, the answer to this question is clearly defined:

5 Strongly Agree

4 Agree

3 Neutral

2 Disagree

1 Strongly Disagree

1. Are there regulatory / compliance issues?
<--- Score

2. How do you take a forward-looking perspective in identifying Research and Development Tax Credit research related to market response and models?
<--- Score

3. Are your goals realistic? Do you need to redefine

your problem? Perhaps the problem has changed or maybe you have reached your goal and need to set a new one?
<--- Score

4. How do you assess your Research and Development Tax Credit workforce capability and capacity needs, including skills, competencies, and staffing levels?
<--- Score

5. As a sponsor, customer or management, how important is it to meet goals, objectives?
<--- Score

6. What is the smallest subset of the problem you can usefully solve?
<--- Score

7. Who defines the rules in relation to any given issue?
<--- Score

8. What else needs to be measured?
<--- Score

9. How much are sponsors, customers, partners, stakeholders involved in Research and Development Tax Credit? In other words, what are the risks, if Research and Development Tax Credit does not deliver successfully?
<--- Score

10. Which information does the Research and Development Tax Credit business case need to include?
<--- Score

11. Are employees recognized for desired behaviors?
<--- Score

12. How do you better involve local users to make sure that R&D that is undertaken addresses local needs and considers local issues?
<--- Score

13. Does there need to be a trade-off between financial sustainability and social objectives?
<--- Score

14. How can the value of your organization or an asset be properly identified?
<--- Score

15. Do you typically bring in technology that leverages core R&D capabilities, or does it feel more like outsourcing non-core needs?
<--- Score

16. Consider your own Research and Development Tax Credit project, what types of organizational problems do you think might be causing or affecting your problem, based on the work done so far?
<--- Score

17. Who else hopes to benefit from it?
<--- Score

18. What is the extent or complexity of the Research and Development Tax Credit problem?
<--- Score

19. Looking at each person individually – does every one have the qualities which are needed to work in

this group?
<--- Score

20. Are there any specific expectations or concerns about the Research and Development Tax Credit team, Research and Development Tax Credit itself?
<--- Score

21. What are the expected benefits of Research and Development Tax Credit to the stakeholder?
<--- Score

22. What are the metrics you would need?
<--- Score

23. What is the problem that is intended to be solved by the research?
<--- Score

24. What does Research and Development Tax Credit success mean to the stakeholders?
<--- Score

25. Are you dealing with any of the same issues today as yesterday? What can you do about this?
<--- Score

26. Will a response program recognize when a crisis occurs and provide some level of response?
<--- Score

27. Are losses recognized in a timely manner?
<--- Score

28. What needs to be done?
<--- Score

29. Does filing an R&D credit trigger an audit?
<--- Score

30. What skills do you think might be needed in the future?
<--- Score

31. Who did you consult, how were corresponding people selected and identified, and how did you run your consultations?
<--- Score

32. Does the problem have ethical dimensions?
<--- Score

33. Can management personnel recognize the monetary benefit of Research and Development Tax Credit?
<--- Score

34. What information do users need?
<--- Score

35. Do you need to avoid or amend any Research and Development Tax Credit activities?
<--- Score

36. What kind of policy approach is needed?
<--- Score

37. What are the stakeholder objectives to be achieved with Research and Development Tax Credit?
<--- Score

38. What Research and Development Tax Credit

coordination do you need?

<--- Score

39. Can you identify expenditure incurred or assets used in the activities?

<--- Score

40. To what level of satisfaction are your technology needs met by your internal R&D?

<--- Score

41. What training and capacity building actions are needed to implement proposed reforms?

<--- Score

42. Who needs to know about Research and Development Tax Credit?

<--- Score

43. What situation(s) led to this Research and Development Tax Credit Self Assessment?

<--- Score

44. When does your organization need to have the requisite purpose?

<--- Score

45. What are the key issues?

<--- Score

46. What would happen if Research and Development Tax Credit weren't done?

<--- Score

47. Does Research and Development Tax Credit create potential expectations in other areas that need to be

recognized and considered?
<--- Score

48. What vendors make products that address the Research and Development Tax Credit needs?
<--- Score

49. How are you going to measure success?
<--- Score

50. How are the Research and Development Tax Credit's objectives aligned to the group's overall stakeholder strategy?
<--- Score

51. What is the problem and/or vulnerability?
<--- Score

52. What needs to stay?
<--- Score

53. What time sensitive issues should you consider in order to not miss any tax savings?
<--- Score

54. What problems are you facing and how do you consider Research and Development Tax Credit will circumvent those obstacles?
<--- Score

Add up total points for this section:
_ _ _ _ _ = Total points for this section

Divided by: _ _ _ _ _ _ (number of statements answered) = _ _ _ _ _ _
Average score for this section

Transfer your score to the Research and Development Tax Credit Index at the beginning of the Self-Assessment.

CRITERION #2: DEFINE:

INTENT: Formulate the stakeholder problem. Define the problem, needs and objectives.

In my belief, the answer to this question is clearly defined:

5 Strongly Agree

4 Agree

3 Neutral

2 Disagree

1 Strongly Disagree

1. Has/have the customer(s) been identified?
<--- Score

2. Do you have organizational privacy requirements?
<--- Score

3. Is data collected and displayed to better understand customer(s) critical needs and requirements.
<--- Score

4. What intelligence can you gather?
<--- Score

5. What is the worst case scenario?
<--- Score

6. Are there any constraints known that bear on the ability to perform Research and Development Tax Credit work? How is the team addressing them?
<--- Score

7. What happens if Research and Development Tax Credit's scope changes?
<--- Score

8. Have the customer needs been translated into specific, measurable requirements? How?
<--- Score

9. What critical content must be communicated – who, what, when, where, and how?
<--- Score

10. How can the value of Research and Development Tax Credit be defined?
<--- Score

11. Are there different segments of customers?
<--- Score

12. Is Research and Development Tax Credit linked to key stakeholder goals and objectives?
<--- Score

13. What are the requirements for audit information?

<--- Score

14. If substitutes have been appointed, have they been briefed on the Research and Development Tax Credit goals and received regular communications as to the progress to date?
<--- Score

15. Has a Research and Development Tax Credit requirement not been met?
<--- Score

16. What are the core elements of the Research and Development Tax Credit business case?
<--- Score

17. Has a team charter been developed and communicated?
<--- Score

18. What would be the goal or target for a Research and Development Tax Credit's improvement team?
<--- Score

19. What are the dynamics of the communication plan?
<--- Score

20. What information do you gather?
<--- Score

21. What specifically is the problem? Where does it occur? When does it occur? What is its extent?
<--- Score

22. What customer feedback methods were used to

solicit their input?

<--- Score

23. When are meeting minutes sent out? Who is on the distribution list?

<--- Score

24. What are the Research and Development Tax Credit use cases?

<--- Score

25. What is the right level of information required to support a claim?

<--- Score

26. Is the team sponsored by a champion or stakeholder leader?

<--- Score

27. Is there a critical path to deliver Research and Development Tax Credit results?

<--- Score

28. What is the scope of Research and Development Tax Credit?

<--- Score

29. How do you manage unclear Research and Development Tax Credit requirements?

<--- Score

30. Will team members regularly document their Research and Development Tax Credit work?

<--- Score

31. What level of resources is required to

implement the new technology?
<--- Score

32. How is the team tracking and documenting its work?
<--- Score

33. Has anyone else (internal or external to the group) attempted to solve this problem or a similar one before? If so, what knowledge can be leveraged from these previous efforts?
<--- Score

34. What defines best in class?
<--- Score

35. Is there a Research and Development Tax Credit management charter, including stakeholder case, problem and goal statements, scope, milestones, roles and responsibilities, communication plan?
<--- Score

36. What are your requirements?
<--- Score

37. Is full participation by members in regularly held team meetings guaranteed?
<--- Score

38. What system do you use for gathering Research and Development Tax Credit information?
<--- Score

39. How do you hand over Research and Development Tax Credit context?
<--- Score

40. What are the compelling stakeholder reasons for embarking on Research and Development Tax Credit?
<--- Score

41. Has everyone on the team, including the team leaders, been properly trained?
<--- Score

42. Do the problem and goal statements meet the SMART criteria (specific, measurable, attainable, relevant, and time-bound)?
<--- Score

43. Was there a prior research credit examination?
<--- Score

44. Has the Research and Development Tax Credit work been fairly and/or equitably divided and delegated among team members who are qualified and capable to perform the work? Has everyone contributed?
<--- Score

45. Is the team formed and are team leaders (Coaches and Management Leads) assigned?
<--- Score

46. What is the Business-Use Requirement?
<--- Score

47. Is it clearly defined in and to your organization what you do?
<--- Score

48. What constraints exist that might impact the

team?
<--- Score

49. Who is gathering information?
<--- Score

50. What key stakeholder process output measure(s) does Research and Development Tax Credit leverage and how?
<--- Score

51. Has the improvement team collected the 'voice of the customer' (obtained feedback – qualitative and quantitative)?
<--- Score

52. Who are the Research and Development Tax Credit improvement team members, including Management Leads and Coaches?
<--- Score

53. When is/was the Research and Development Tax Credit start date?
<--- Score

54. What are the boundaries of the scope? What is in bounds and what is not? What is the start point? What is the stop point?
<--- Score

55. What are the rough order estimates on cost savings/opportunities that Research and Development Tax Credit brings?
<--- Score

56. Are required metrics defined, what are they?

<--- Score

57. What Research and Development Tax Credit services do you require?
<--- Score

58. Are different versions of process maps needed to account for the different types of inputs?
<--- Score

59. Are improvement team members fully trained on Research and Development Tax Credit?
<--- Score

60. Is Research and Development Tax Credit currently on schedule according to the plan?
<--- Score

61. How do you keep key subject matter experts in the loop?
<--- Score

62. The political context: who holds power?
<--- Score

63. What are the requirements for eligible R&D activities?
<--- Score

64. How will variation in the actual durations of each activity be dealt with to ensure that the expected Research and Development Tax Credit results are met?
<--- Score

65. Who is gathering Research and Development Tax Credit information?

<--- Score

66. How will the Research and Development Tax Credit team and the group measure complete success of Research and Development Tax Credit?
<--- Score

67. Is there a completed SIPOC representation, describing the Suppliers, Inputs, Process, Outputs, and Customers?
<--- Score

68. Is the team adequately staffed with the desired cross-functionality? If not, what additional resources are available to the team?
<--- Score

69. What are the Roles and Responsibilities for each team member and its leadership? Where is this documented?
<--- Score

70. Scope of sensitive information?
<--- Score

71. Is there regularly 100% attendance at the team meetings? If not, have appointed substitutes attended to preserve cross-functionality and full representation?
<--- Score

72. Will team members perform Research and Development Tax Credit work when assigned and in a timely fashion?
<--- Score

73. Is the Research and Development Tax Credit scope manageable?

<--- Score

74. What scope do you want your strategy to cover?

<--- Score

75. How was the 'as is' process map developed, reviewed, verified and validated?

<--- Score

76. Has a project plan, Gantt chart, or similar been developed/completed?

<--- Score

77. Are team charters developed?

<--- Score

78. Is the current 'as is' process being followed? If not, what are the discrepancies?

<--- Score

79. Is special Research and Development Tax Credit user knowledge required?

<--- Score

80. What is the scope of the review?

<--- Score

81. How did the Research and Development Tax Credit manager receive input to the development of a Research and Development Tax Credit improvement plan and the estimated completion dates/times of each activity?

<--- Score

82. Has a high-level 'as is' process map been completed, verified and validated?
<--- Score

83. What is the scope of the Research and Development Tax Credit effort?
<--- Score

84. When is the estimated completion date?
<--- Score

85. Are roles and responsibilities formally defined?
<--- Score

86. Is there a completed, verified, and validated high-level 'as is' (not 'should be' or 'could be') stakeholder process map?
<--- Score

87. Is the improvement team aware of the different versions of a process: what they think it is vs. what it actually is vs. what it should be vs. what it could be?
<--- Score

88. Is the team equipped with available and reliable resources?
<--- Score

89. How often are the team meetings?
<--- Score

90. How does the Research and Development Tax Credit manager ensure against scope creep?
<--- Score

91. Are customer(s) identified and segmented

according to their different needs and requirements?
<--- Score

92. Has the direction changed at all during the course of Research and Development Tax Credit? If so, when did it change and why?
<--- Score

93. In what way can you redefine the criteria of choice clients have in your category in your favor?
<--- Score

94. Are customers identified and high impact areas defined?
<--- Score

95. How do you gather the stories?
<--- Score

96. How do you manage scope?
<--- Score

97. Are you required to provide contemporaneous support?
<--- Score

98. Is a fully trained team formed, supported, and committed to work on the Research and Development Tax Credit improvements?
<--- Score

99. Are stakeholder processes mapped?
<--- Score

100. Does the team have regular meetings?
<--- Score

Add up total points for this section:

_____ = Total points for this section

Divided by: _____ (number of
statements answered) = _____
Average score for this section

Transfer your score to the Research and
Development Tax Credit Index at the
beginning of the Self-Assessment.

CRITERION #3: MEASURE:

INTENT: Gather the correct data.
Measure the current performance and
evolution of the situation.

In my belief, the answer to this
question is clearly defined:

5 Strongly Agree

4 Agree

3 Neutral

2 Disagree

1 Strongly Disagree

1. Do subsidies have positive impacts on R&D and innovation activities at your organization level?
<--- Score

2. Do you understand how to quantify the potential benefit?
<--- Score

3. What are you verifying?

<--- Score

4. What key measures identified indicate the performance of the stakeholder process?
<--- Score

5. How do you measure lifecycle phases?
<--- Score

6. Does the cost of an audit outweigh the benefit of the tax incentive?
<--- Score

7. What can be said about the overall impact of the credit on domestic R&D?
<--- Score

8. How to cause the change?
<--- Score

9. How has tax affected the changing cost of R&D?
<--- Score

10. How do your measurements capture actionable Research and Development Tax Credit information for use in exceeding your customers expectations and securing your customers engagement?
<--- Score

11. What particular quality tools did the team find helpful in establishing measurements?
<--- Score

12. What happens if cost savings do not materialize?
<--- Score

13. Is a solid data collection plan established that includes measurement systems analysis?
<--- Score

14. R&D consortia impact on competitiveness?
<--- Score

15. What are the agreed upon definitions of the high impact areas, defect(s), unit(s), and opportunities that will figure into the process capability metrics?
<--- Score

16. What is the right balance of time and resources between investigation, analysis, and discussion and dissemination?
<--- Score

17. How frequently do you track Research and Development Tax Credit measures?
<--- Score

18. How are labor costs tracked for internal employees?
<--- Score

19. Have you quantified the value of R&D tax credits to your business?
<--- Score

20. How will effects be measured?
<--- Score

21. Are the different measures substitutes or complements?
<--- Score

22. How do you measure efficient delivery of Research and Development Tax Credit services?
<--- Score

23. Can the cost of the R&D Tax Incentive program be better understood and estimated?
<--- Score

24. Are key measures identified and agreed upon?
<--- Score

25. Is data collected on key measures that were identified?
<--- Score

26. What do people want to verify?
<--- Score

27. Is long term and short term variability accounted for?
<--- Score

28. Has the economic impact of a project been accurately detailed?
<--- Score

29. How will your organization measure success?
<--- Score

30. Which Research and Development Tax Credit impacts are significant?
<--- Score

31. What measurements are possible, practicable and meaningful?
<--- Score

32. Does Research and Development Tax Credit analysis show the relationships among important Research and Development Tax Credit factors?
<--- Score

33. What evidence is there and what is measured?
<--- Score

34. Was a data collection plan established?
<--- Score

35. Are there differences between measures with respect to what type of R&D is carried out?
<--- Score

36. How do you measure market effects?
<--- Score

37. Are you aware of what could cause a problem?
<--- Score

38. Have you found any 'ground fruit' or 'low-hanging fruit' for immediate remedies to the gap in performance?
<--- Score

39. How is progress measured?
<--- Score

40. R&D productivity: how should it be measured?
<--- Score

41. Who pays the cost?
<--- Score

42. What are the costs of reform?
<--- Score

43. What has the team done to assure the stability and accuracy of the measurement process?
<--- Score

44. What are the current costs of the Research and Development Tax Credit process?
<--- Score

45. What is the context in which you are making decisions about R&D, what are priorities?
<--- Score

46. Is data collection planned and executed?
<--- Score

47. Who should receive measurement reports?
<--- Score

48. Are the Research and Development Tax Credit benefits worth its costs?
<--- Score

49. How do you verify Research and Development Tax Credit completeness and accuracy?
<--- Score

50. What are the estimated costs of proposed changes?
<--- Score

51. Are there competing Research and Development Tax Credit priorities?
<--- Score

52. What are the key input variables? What are the key process variables? What are the key output variables?
<--- Score

53. What causes innovation to fail or succeed in your organization?
<--- Score

54. What if R&D expenses increase because of a merger, acquisition or reorganization?
<--- Score

55. What are eligible R&D Costs?
<--- Score

56. Do you verify that corrective actions were taken?
<--- Score

57. Where can you go to verify the info?
<--- Score

58. Is it possible to estimate the impact of unanticipated complexity such as wrong or failed assumptions, feedback, etcetera on proposed reforms?
<--- Score

59. What is the impact of government support for business R&D?
<--- Score

60. How do you verify the authenticity of the data and information used?
<--- Score

61. What measures is the Minister of State taking to encourage women in business?

<--- Score

62. Which costs qualify for R&D tax relief?

<--- Score

63. Does Research and Development Tax Credit systematically track and analyze outcomes for accountability and quality improvement?

<--- Score

64. What causes mismanagement?

<--- Score

65. Is key measure data collection planned and executed, process variation displayed and communicated and performance baselined?

<--- Score

66. How do you verify the Research and Development Tax Credit requirements quality?

<--- Score

67. What are your primary costs, revenues, assets?

<--- Score

68. What could cause delays in the schedule?

<--- Score

69. Are there any easy-to-implement alternatives to Research and Development Tax Credit? Sometimes other solutions are available that do not require the cost implications of a full-blown project?

<--- Score

70. Have the types of risks that may impact Research and Development Tax Credit been identified and analyzed?
<--- Score

71. Which costs should be taken into account?
<--- Score

72. What would be a real cause for concern?
<--- Score

73. How are you addressing the new priorities?
<--- Score

74. How large is the gap between current performance and the customer-specified (goal) performance?
<--- Score

75. Have you made assumptions about the shape of the future, particularly its impact on your customers and competitors?
<--- Score

76. Do you have an issue in getting priority?
<--- Score

77. Are high impact defects defined and identified in the stakeholder process?
<--- Score

78. Is there a Performance Baseline?
<--- Score

79. What is your Research and Development Tax Credit quality cost segregation study?

<--- Score

80. Will the credit enhance the likelihood of developing products that have important public impact?
<--- Score

81. What are the uncertainties surrounding estimates of impact?
<--- Score

82. Is Process Variation Displayed/Communicated?
<--- Score

83. What are the reform priorities?
<--- Score

84. Have all non-recommended alternatives been analyzed in sufficient detail?
<--- Score

85. What is the root cause(s) of the problem?
<--- Score

86. What causes investor action?
<--- Score

87. Are process variation components displayed/ communicated using suitable charts, graphs, plots?
<--- Score

88. Where is the cost?
<--- Score

89. Where is it measured?
<--- Score

90. Are you taking your company in the direction of better and revenue or cheaper and cost?
<--- Score

91. Are there measurements based on task performance?
<--- Score

92. How can you reduce the costs of obtaining inputs?
<--- Score

93. What are the real costs of the R&D tax incentive to the government?
<--- Score

94. What data was collected (past, present, future/ongoing)?
<--- Score

95. What costs do not qualify?
<--- Score

96. Do the benefits outweigh the costs?
<--- Score

97. What charts has the team used to display the components of variation in the process?
<--- Score

98. What details are required of the Research and Development Tax Credit cost structure?
<--- Score

99. How can you measure Research and Development Tax Credit in a systematic way?

<--- Score

100. Who participated in the data collection for measurements?
<--- Score

101. Will Research and Development Tax Credit have an impact on current business continuity, disaster recovery processes and/or infrastructure?
<--- Score

102. Do you carry out testing, analysis and research?
<--- Score

Add up total points for this section:
_ _ _ _ _ = Total points for this section

Divided by: _ _ _ _ _ _ (number of statements answered) = _ _ _ _ _ _
Average score for this section

Transfer your score to the Research and Development Tax Credit Index at the beginning of the Self-Assessment.

CRITERION #4: ANALYZE:

INTENT: Analyze causes, assumptions and hypotheses.

In my belief, the answer to this question is clearly defined:

5 Strongly Agree

4 Agree

3 Neutral

2 Disagree

1 Strongly Disagree

1. Were Pareto charts (or similar) used to portray the 'heavy hitters' (or key sources of variation)?
<--- Score

2. Was a detailed process map created to amplify critical steps of the 'as is' stakeholder process?
<--- Score

3. Think about the functions involved in your Research and Development Tax Credit project, what processes

flow from these functions?
<--- Score

4. Did any additional data need to be collected?
<--- Score

5. Think about some of the processes you undertake within your organization, which do you own?
<--- Score

6. What number of miles qualify as a deductible travel expense?
<--- Score

7. How was the detailed process map generated, verified, and validated?
<--- Score

8. What controls do you have in place to protect data?
<--- Score

9. What types of research expenses qualify?
<--- Score

10. How much data can be collected in the given timeframe?
<--- Score

11. Who qualifies for the R&D tax credit?
<--- Score

12. What are the qualified research expenses (QRE) for the R&D Credit?
<--- Score

13. What output to create?

<--- Score

14. Can you add value to the current Research and Development Tax Credit decision-making process (largely qualitative) by incorporating uncertainty modeling (more quantitative)?
<--- Score

15. What constitutes qualified research?
<--- Score

16. Where is Research and Development Tax Credit data gathered?
<--- Score

17. What is the process of preparing and approving financial submissions?
<--- Score

18. Can you amend a prior year return to claim a qualified R&D Credit?
<--- Score

19. What, related to, Research and Development Tax Credit processes does your organization outsource?
<--- Score

20. Have the problem and goal statements been updated to reflect the additional knowledge gained from the analyze phase?
<--- Score

21. What is the cost of poor quality as supported by the team's analysis?
<--- Score

22. How do you measure the operational performance of your key work systems and processes, including productivity, cycle time, and other appropriate measures of process effectiveness, efficiency, and innovation?
<--- Score

23. What is your organizations system for selecting qualified vendors?
<--- Score

24. How do mission and objectives affect the Research and Development Tax Credit processes of your organization?
<--- Score

25. What qualifications do Research and Development Tax Credit leaders need?
<--- Score

26. What tools were used to narrow the list of possible causes?
<--- Score

27. What are the shortcomings of the actual data situation?
<--- Score

28. Does the research involve a process of experimentation?
<--- Score

29. How is the way you as the leader think and process information affecting your organizational culture?
<--- Score

30. What qualifies as competition?
<--- Score

31. Have any additional benefits been identified that will result from closing all or most of the gaps?
<--- Score

32. Is the gap/opportunity displayed and communicated in financial terms?
<--- Score

33. Have you defined which data is gathered how?
<--- Score

34. How will the change process be managed?
<--- Score

35. Is there a strict change management process?
<--- Score

36. What internal processes need improvement?
<--- Score

37. What research activities do not qualify for R&D Credit?
<--- Score

38. How can consulting engineers and mechanical contractors qualify for the credit?
<--- Score

39. What are your current levels and trends in key measures or indicators of Research and Development Tax Credit product and process performance that are important to and directly serve your customers? How do these results compare with the performance of

your competitors and other organizations with similar offerings?
<--- Score

40. Are Research and Development Tax Credit changes recognized early enough to be approved through the regular process?
<--- Score

41. What were the financial benefits resulting from any 'ground fruit or low-hanging fruit' (quick fixes)?
<--- Score

42. Are gaps between current performance and the goal performance identified?
<--- Score

43. How are outputs preserved and protected?
<--- Score

44. What expenses qualify for the R&D tax credit?
<--- Score

45. What were the crucial 'moments of truth' on the process map?
<--- Score

46. What kind of crime could a potential new hire have committed that would not only not disqualify him/her from being hired by your organization, but would actually indicate that he/she might be a particularly good fit?
<--- Score

47. Will your business qualify for R&D tax credits?
<--- Score

48. What is a Qualifying Research Activity (QRAs)?
<--- Score

49. Is the R&D tax incentive the right vehicle to drive business innovation?
<--- Score

50. What is qualified research for the income tax credit?
<--- Score

51. Is data and process analysis, root cause analysis and quantifying the gap/opportunity in place?
<--- Score

52. What elements of your projects qualify as R&D?
<--- Score

53. Do you need to examine the process to produce better links to innovation and enterprise?
<--- Score

54. Do process improvements still qualify for the R&D tax credit?
<--- Score

55. What is qualified research?
<--- Score

56. Who will gather what data?
<--- Score

57. Who does not qualify for the credit?
<--- Score

58. What activities & who qualifies?

<--- Score

59. What are the Research and Development Tax Credit business drivers?

<--- Score

60. Is the process formal/informal?

<--- Score

61. Who gets your output?

<--- Score

62. What are your outputs?

<--- Score

63. Does testing qualify for R&D tax relief?

<--- Score

64. What activities qualify for the R&D tax credit?

<--- Score

65. What is the Research and Development Tax Credit Driver?

<--- Score

66. Did any value-added analysis or 'lean thinking' take place to identify some of the gaps shown on the 'as is' process map?

<--- Score

67. What expenses qualify?

<--- Score

68. What do you need to qualify?

<--- Score

69. Do you have the authority to produce the output?
<--- Score

70. What major elements would you include in an R&D organizations strategy process?
<--- Score

71. What activities qualify?
<--- Score

72. What is a qualified activity?
<--- Score

73. Is the commoditization of data in your future?
<--- Score

74. Who and what qualifies for the R&D credit?
<--- Score

75. What types of expenses qualify for the credit calculation?
<--- Score

76. An organizationally feasible system request is one that considers the mission, goals and objectives of the organization, key questions are: is the Research and Development Tax Credit solution request practical and will it solve a problem or take advantage of an opportunity to achieve company goals?
<--- Score

77. Who owns what data?
<--- Score

78. What research expenses qualify for the credit?

<--- Score

79. Has the introduction of the scheme resulted in a change in organizations R&D decision process?
<--- Score

80. How do you implement and manage your work processes to ensure that they meet design requirements?
<--- Score

81. Is your organization developing new or improved products or processes?
<--- Score

82. What is the process or order of the decision?
<--- Score

83. Were there any improvement opportunities identified from the process analysis?
<--- Score

84. Is the required Research and Development Tax Credit data gathered?
<--- Score

85. Does your organization take on projects related to developing a new product or process or improving upon an existing one?
<--- Score

86. What other jobs or tasks affect the performance of the steps in the Research and Development Tax Credit process?
<--- Score

87. Creativity is central to many activities, including entrepreneurship and research and development at large corporations. Can incentives be used to improve the creative process?
<--- Score

88. Is strict confidentiality maintained in the receipt and processing of reports?
<--- Score

89. Do you qualify?
<--- Score

90. What tools were used to generate the list of possible causes?
<--- Score

91. Is the performance gap determined?
<--- Score

92. Are patents more or less effective than secrecy in protecting process innovations from duplication?
<--- Score

93. Was a cause-and-effect diagram used to explore the different types of causes (or sources of variation)?
<--- Score

94. What Research and Development Tax Credit data should be collected?
<--- Score

95. How do you promote understanding that opportunity for improvement is not criticism of the status quo, or the people who created the status quo?

<--- Score

96. What is a qualified tax credit activity?
<--- Score

97. What qualifies as research?
<--- Score

98. Which projects qualify?
<--- Score

99. Were any designed experiments used to generate additional insight into the data analysis?
<--- Score

100. Record-keeping requirements flow from the records needed as inputs, outputs, controls and for transformation of a Research and Development Tax Credit process, are the records needed as inputs to the Research and Development Tax Credit process available?
<--- Score

101. Is the Research and Development Tax Credit process severely broken such that a re-design is necessary?
<--- Score

102. Is your product/process seeking to achieve an advance in science or technology?
<--- Score

103. What does the data say about the performance of the stakeholder process?
<--- Score

104. From design to development - what qualifies?
<--- Score

105. What are the revised rough estimates of the financial savings/opportunity for Research and Development Tax Credit improvements?
<--- Score

106. Are all team members qualified for all tasks?
<--- Score

107. What types of research qualify for the credit?
<--- Score

108. Do your contracts/agreements contain data security obligations?
<--- Score

109. Who qualifies to gain access to data?
<--- Score

110. How is the data gathered?
<--- Score

111. Who can qualify for the credit?
<--- Score

112. What drives venture capital fundraising?
<--- Score

113. Is the final output clearly identified?
<--- Score

114. How many input/output points does it require?
<--- Score

115. What are the possible data sources?
<--- Score

116. What process should you select for improvement?
<--- Score

117. Does your organizations project qualify?
<--- Score

118. What is qualified research and development?
<--- Score

119. Are you innovating and/or improving processes, product or a service?
<--- Score

120. Are all staff in core Research and Development Tax Credit subjects Highly Qualified?
<--- Score

121. Are you conducting a process of experimentation?
<--- Score

122. What is qualified research for R&D Credit?
<--- Score

123. Is employee data being protected?
<--- Score

124. Are there additional opportunities beyond the traditional R&D tax credit?
<--- Score

125. Who qualifies for the credit?

<--- Score

126. Does the project qualify as an early-mover innovation?
<--- Score

127. What did the team gain from developing a sub-process map?
<--- Score

128. What conclusions were drawn from the team's data collection and analysis? How did the team reach these conclusions?
<--- Score

129. What quality tools were used to get through the analyze phase?
<--- Score

130. What is the output?
<--- Score

Add up total points for this section:
_ _ _ _ _ = Total points for this section

Divided by: _ _ _ _ _ _ (number of statements answered) = _ _ _ _ _ _
Average score for this section

Transfer your score to the Research and Development Tax Credit Index at the beginning of the Self-Assessment.

CRITERION #5: IMPROVE:

INTENT: Develop a practical solution. Innovate, establish and test the solution and to measure the results.

In my belief, the answer to this question is clearly defined:

5 Strongly Agree

4 Agree

3 Neutral

2 Disagree

1 Strongly Disagree

1. Is there a documentation requirement?
<--- Score

2. How can you better manage risk?
<--- Score

3. Is there a small-scale pilot for proposed improvement(s)? What conclusions were drawn from the outcomes of a pilot?

<--- Score

4. Is the optimal solution selected based on testing and analysis?
<--- Score

5. What tools were used to tap into the creativity and encourage 'outside the box' thinking?
<--- Score

6. How do you manage and improve your Research and Development Tax Credit work systems to deliver customer value and achieve organizational success and sustainability?
<--- Score

7. Will the development be used in the internal administration of your business or that of an affiliate?
<--- Score

8. Jobs and taxes: do state taxes affect economic development?
<--- Score

9. How will the team or the process owner(s) monitor the implementation plan to see that it is working as intended?
<--- Score

10. What is the frequency and timeframe of R&D decisions?
<--- Score

11. When is the research and development (R&D) tax credit being repealed from?

<--- Score

12. What Research and Development Tax Credit improvements can be made?
<--- Score

13. How do you improve your likelihood of success ?
<--- Score

14. How can skill-level changes improve Research and Development Tax Credit?
<--- Score

15. Should government back community development organizations?
<--- Score

16. How will the group know that the solution worked?
<--- Score

17. Do your activities meet the 4-part test for research and development?
<--- Score

18. Can you claim for website or app development?
<--- Score

19. Describe the design of the pilot and what tests were conducted, if any?
<--- Score

20. Is the implementation plan designed?
<--- Score

21. What factors do you consider in making

decisions about R&D?

<--- Score

22. Which research results can be commercialized and by whom?

<--- Score

23. How scalable is your Research and Development Tax Credit solution?

<--- Score

24. What strategies for Research and Development Tax Credit improvement are successful?

<--- Score

25. Which incentives should be evaluated?

<--- Score

26. Is pilot data collected and analyzed?

<--- Score

27. Are there any other risks that need to be managed?

<--- Score

28. How can the phases of Research and Development Tax Credit development be identified?

<--- Score

29. How can the tax incentive program best be evaluated in the future?

<--- Score

30. Are you assessing Research and Development Tax Credit and risk?

<--- Score

31. How do you go about comparing Research and Development Tax Credit approaches/solutions?
<--- Score

32. Do those selected for the Research and Development Tax Credit team have a good general understanding of what Research and Development Tax Credit is all about?
<--- Score

33. Which Research and Development Tax Credit solution is appropriate?
<--- Score

34. Are the best solutions selected?
<--- Score

35. How do you deal with Research and Development Tax Credit risk?
<--- Score

36. Is there a cost/benefit analysis of optimal solution(s)?
<--- Score

37. To which extent can research and development activities be supported?
<--- Score

38. Is the Research and Development Tax Credit documentation thorough?
<--- Score

39. What were the criteria for evaluating a Research and Development Tax Credit pilot?

<--- Score

40. Risk factors: what are the characteristics of Research and Development Tax Credit that make it risky?
<--- Score

41. How do you improve knowledge transfer and application?
<--- Score

42. How is knowledge integrated, sourced and recombined from internal and external sources for innovation and new product development?
<--- Score

43. Is there a federal award for research and development?
<--- Score

44. Are new and improved process ('should be') maps developed?
<--- Score

45. How do you define the solutions' scope?
<--- Score

46. How do you measure progress and evaluate training effectiveness?
<--- Score

47. How does the solution remove the key sources of issues discovered in the analyze phase?
<--- Score

48. What are your current levels and trends in key

measures or indicators of workforce and leader development?

<--- Score

49. Are possible solutions generated and tested?

<--- Score

50. What error proofing will be done to address some of the discrepancies observed in the 'as is' process?

<--- Score

51. Who is involved in making decisions about R&D and how does it work?

<--- Score

52. Where do you need Research and Development Tax Credit improvement?

<--- Score

53. What are the specific documentation requirements for the R&D Credit?

<--- Score

54. What decisions can be reviewed?

<--- Score

55. Are you undertaking software development activities?

<--- Score

56. What are the specific documentation requirements for the your states R&D Credit?

<--- Score

57. Have you achieved Research and Development Tax Credit improvements?

<--- Score

58. Who controls the risk?
<--- Score

59. What needs improvement? Why?
<--- Score

60. Do they care how much time it takes to achieve the desired result?
<--- Score

61. Research and development at your organization level: does the source of financing matter?
<--- Score

62. Is a contingency plan established?
<--- Score

63. How do you make decisions about investments (in general) and R&D in particular?
<--- Score

64. What is the Research and Development Tax Credit's sustainability risk?
<--- Score

65. What lessons, if any, from a pilot were incorporated into the design of the full-scale solution?
<--- Score

66. How do you decide what R&D to conduct?
<--- Score

67. What communications are necessary to support

the implementation of the solution?
<--- Score

68. How do you link measurement and risk?
<--- Score

69. What is the team's contingency plan for potential problems occurring in implementation?
<--- Score

70. Who benefits from economic development incentives?
<--- Score

71. When does design become research and development?
<--- Score

72. Investment in research and development - does tax policy matter?
<--- Score

73. Did an outside consultant provide a research and development study?
<--- Score

74. What is sufficient documentation?
<--- Score

75. Are risk triggers captured?
<--- Score

76. What tools were most useful during the improve phase?
<--- Score

77. Who is involved in making decisions about R&D?
<--- Score

78. How do you decide how much to remunerate an employee?
<--- Score

79. In the past few months, what is the smallest change you have made that has had the biggest positive result? What was it about that small change that produced the large return?
<--- Score

80. Is private sector research and development increasing?
<--- Score

81. Is a solution implementation plan established, including schedule/work breakdown structure, resources, risk management plan, cost/budget, and control plan?
<--- Score

82. Can you claim for market research and business case development?
<--- Score

83. How can you improve Research and Development Tax Credit?
<--- Score

84. What improvements have been achieved?
<--- Score

85. Is supporting Research and Development Tax

Credit documentation required?

<--- Score

86. Are new technological developments required for the success of the initiative?

<--- Score

87. Have you conducted software development activities?

<--- Score

88. Who benefits from state and local economic development policies?

<--- Score

89. What are the expected Research and Development Tax Credit results?

<--- Score

90. How do you improve Research and Development Tax Credit service perception, and satisfaction?

<--- Score

91. What documentation must be kept?

<--- Score

92. Can you use the credit to offset the economic development surcharge?

<--- Score

93. What is the implementation plan?

<--- Score

94. What is Research and Development Tax Credit's impact on utilizing the best solution(s)?

<--- Score

95. How are R&D project investment decisions made?
<--- Score

96. How did the team generate the list of possible solutions?
<--- Score

97. What attendant changes will need to be made to ensure that the solution is successful?
<--- Score

98. Was a pilot designed for the proposed solution(s)?
<--- Score

99. Are decisions made in a timely manner?
<--- Score

100. Were any criteria developed to assist the team in testing and evaluating potential solutions?
<--- Score

101. What tools were used to evaluate the potential solutions?
<--- Score

102. Is the R&D tax incentive program well understood by stakeholders and easy to access?
<--- Score

103. How do you measure improved Research and Development Tax Credit service perception, and satisfaction?
<--- Score

104. What were the underlying assumptions on the cost-benefit analysis?
<--- Score

105. If you could go back in time five years, what decision would you make differently? What is your best guess as to what decision you're making today you might regret five years from now?
<--- Score

106. Are there any constraints (technical, political, cultural, or otherwise) that would inhibit certain solutions?
<--- Score

107. What does the 'should be' process map/design look like?
<--- Score

108. Is research and development occurring?
<--- Score

109. Describe your organizations approach to research and development?
<--- Score

110. Are improved process ('should be') maps modified based on pilot data and analysis?
<--- Score

111. What is your decision requirements diagram?
<--- Score

112. Does the existence of R&D grants influence decision making?
<--- Score

113. How will you know that a change is an improvement?
<--- Score

114. Who controls key decisions that will be made?
<--- Score

115. Who will be using the results of the measurement activities?
<--- Score

116. Does the existence of R&D tax credits influence decision making?
<--- Score

Add up total points for this section:
_ _ _ _ _ = Total points for this section

Divided by: _ _ _ _ _ _ (number of statements answered) = _ _ _ _ _ _
Average score for this section

Transfer your score to the Research and Development Tax Credit Index at the beginning of the Self-Assessment.

CRITERION #6: CONTROL:

INTENT: Implement the practical solution. Maintain the performance and correct possible complications.

In my belief, the answer to this question is clearly defined:

5 Strongly Agree

4 Agree

3 Neutral

2 Disagree

1 Strongly Disagree

1. Are new process steps, standards, and documentation ingrained into normal operations?
<--- Score

2. Will any special training be provided for results interpretation?
<--- Score

3. **Does learning about benefits of R&D lead to**

sustained higher levels of investment?

<--- Score

4. Does a troubleshooting guide exist or is it needed?

<--- Score

5. Are documented procedures clear and easy to follow for the operators?

<--- Score

6. Does Research and Development Tax Credit appropriately measure and monitor risk?

<--- Score

7. Are suggested corrective/restorative actions indicated on the response plan for known causes to problems that might surface?

<--- Score

8. Does your organization review its internal controls regularly enough to cater for changing circumstances?

<--- Score

9. What do you measure to verify effectiveness gains?

<--- Score

10. Is there a transfer of ownership and knowledge to process owner and process team tasked with the responsibilities.

<--- Score

11. What other systems, operations, processes, and infrastructures (hiring practices, staffing, training, incentives/rewards, metrics/dashboards/scorecards, etc.) need updates, additions, changes, or deletions

in order to facilitate knowledge transfer and improvements?

<--- Score

12. Is there a standardized process?

<--- Score

13. What key inputs and outputs are being measured on an ongoing basis?

<--- Score

14. Are operating procedures consistent?

<--- Score

15. Has the improved process and its steps been standardized?

<--- Score

16. How do you select, collect, align, and integrate Research and Development Tax Credit data and information for tracking daily operations and overall organizational performance, including progress relative to strategic objectives and action plans?

<--- Score

17. Will existing staff require re-training, for example, to learn new business processes?

<--- Score

18. How is Research and Development Tax Credit project cost planned, managed, monitored?

<--- Score

19. What are the critical parameters to watch?

<--- Score

20. How will the process owner verify improvement in present and future sigma levels, process capabilities?
<--- Score

21. Does the response plan contain a definite closed loop continual improvement scheme (e.g., plan-do-check-act)?
<--- Score

22. Has the program been monitored by your organization on a regular basis?
<--- Score

23. Does the Research and Development Tax Credit performance meet the customer's requirements?
<--- Score

24. Is there documentation that will support the successful operation of the improvement?
<--- Score

25. How do senior leaders actions reflect a commitment to the organizations Research and Development Tax Credit values?
<--- Score

26. How do you establish and deploy modified action plans if circumstances require a shift in plans and rapid execution of new plans?
<--- Score

27. How will Research and Development Tax Credit decisions be made and monitored?
<--- Score

28. Who controls critical resources?

<--- Score

29. What research and development (R&D) activities are you performing or planning?
<--- Score

30. Are there documented procedures?
<--- Score

31. Who is the Research and Development Tax Credit process owner?
<--- Score

32. What can you control?
<--- Score

33. What do you stand for--and what are you against?
<--- Score

34. What do your reports reflect?
<--- Score

35. What is your theory of human motivation, and how does your compensation plan fit with that view?
<--- Score

36. How will input, process, and output variables be checked to detect for sub-optimal conditions?
<--- Score

37. Is there a documented and implemented monitoring plan?
<--- Score

38. How will report readings be checked to effectively monitor performance?

<--- Score

39. Is the Research and Development Tax Credit test/monitoring cost justified?
<--- Score

40. What are the known security controls?
<--- Score

41. What is the control/monitoring plan?
<--- Score

42. Is there a control plan in place for sustaining improvements (short and long-term)?
<--- Score

43. Does job training on the documented procedures need to be part of the process team's education and training?
<--- Score

44. What other areas of the group might benefit from the Research and Development Tax Credit team's improvements, knowledge, and learning?
<--- Score

45. How will new or emerging customer needs/requirements be checked/communicated to orient the process toward meeting the new specifications and continually reducing variation?
<--- Score

46. Who participates in the planning process?
<--- Score

47. How will the day-to-day responsibilities for

monitoring and continual improvement be transferred from the improvement team to the process owner?
<--- Score

48. Is reporting being used or needed?
<--- Score

49. Are the Research and Development Tax Credit standards challenging?
<--- Score

50. Is knowledge gained on process shared and institutionalized?
<--- Score

51. What should the next improvement project be that is related to Research and Development Tax Credit?
<--- Score

52. How will the process owner and team be able to hold the gains?
<--- Score

53. Where do ideas that reach policy makers and planners as proposals for Research and Development Tax Credit strengthening and reform actually originate?
<--- Score

54. Is there a recommended audit plan for routine surveillance inspections of Research and Development Tax Credit's gains?
<--- Score

55. Have new or revised work instructions resulted?
<--- Score

56. Has your organization conducted site visits to monitor its investment?
<--- Score

57. Do you feel prepared to navigate the process and communicate plans and costs to your employees?
<--- Score

58. How might the group capture best practices and lessons learned so as to leverage improvements?
<--- Score

59. Is a response plan established and deployed?
<--- Score

60. Is new knowledge gained imbedded in the response plan?
<--- Score

61. Does the proposal provide for a way to monitor its success?
<--- Score

62. What is the recommended frequency of auditing?
<--- Score

63. What does statutory requirements and standards cover?
<--- Score

64. How do you encourage people to take control and responsibility?

<--- Score

65. You may have created your quality measures at a time when you lacked resources, technology wasn't up to the required standard, or low service levels were the industry norm. Have those circumstances changed?
<--- Score

66. What is the standard for acceptable Research and Development Tax Credit performance?
<--- Score

67. Is a response plan in place for when the input, process, or output measures indicate an 'out-of-control' condition?
<--- Score

68. Are you measuring, monitoring and predicting Research and Development Tax Credit activities to optimize operations and profitability, and enhancing outcomes?
<--- Score

69. What quality tools were useful in the control phase?
<--- Score

Add up total points for this section:
_ _ _ _ _ = Total points for this section

Divided by: _ _ _ _ _ _ (number of statements answered) = _ _ _ _ _ _
Average score for this section

Transfer your score to the Research and

Development Tax Credit Index at the beginning of the Self-Assessment.

CRITERION #7: SUSTAIN:

INTENT: Retain the benefits.

In my belief, the answer to this question is clearly defined:

5 Strongly Agree

4 Agree

3 Neutral

2 Disagree

1 Strongly Disagree

1. Why is this relevant?
<--- Score

2. Is the program meeting its goals?
<--- Score

3. Do R&D tax incentives lead to higher wages for R&D workers?
<--- Score

4. Does the tax system favor investment in high

tech or smoke-stack industries?

<--- Score

5. Do you think you know, or do you know you know ?

<--- Score

6. Do you build Models/Prototypes?

<--- Score

7. What kinds of R&D do you conduct/have you conducted?

<--- Score

8. How can it deliver significant benefits to companies in the industry?

<--- Score

9. How does the R&D Tax Incentive program compare with international practice?

<--- Score

10. What are strategies for increasing support and reducing opposition?

<--- Score

11. What are the key enablers to make this Research and Development Tax Credit move?

<--- Score

12. Can the schedule be done in the given time?

<--- Score

13. Do tax incentives increase 401(k) retirement saving?

<--- Score

14. Do organizations in your sector make good R&D Tax Credit clients?

<--- Score

15. More R&D = more innovation ?

<--- Score

16. Is the R&D credit a refundable credit?

<--- Score

17. What types of transferrable credits exist?

<--- Score

18. What are the expectations and to what extent are they met?

<--- Score

19. How much should you trust differences-in-differences estimates?

<--- Score

20. How do you provide a safe environment -physically and emotionally?

<--- Score

21. Would the activity have occurred in the absence of the core R&D activity?

<--- Score

22. Will the software be used for the purpose of internal administration?

<--- Score

23. Are there expected spillovers associated with the project?

<--- Score

24. Why hasnt the R&D tax credit been extended again or made permanent?

<--- Score

25. What are the benefits?

<--- Score

26. May the R&D be performed outside the country?

<--- Score

27. Do R&D tax credits create jobs?

<--- Score

28. What work is not eligible?

<--- Score

29. How is tax relief calculated?

<--- Score

30. What trends do you see in the industry?

<--- Score

31. What are the performance and scale of the Research and Development Tax Credit tools?

<--- Score

32. How do you know if you are successful?

<--- Score

33. If you build it, will they fund?

<--- Score

34. Is the tax credit not refundable right from the start?

<--- Score

35. What is the purpose of the credit?
<--- Score

36. Who did the research?
<--- Score

37. What governs firm-level R&D: Internal or external factors?
<--- Score

38. Does the corporation have investments in joint venture(s) or partnership(s)?
<--- Score

39. Is public R&D a complement or a substitute for private R&D?
<--- Score

40. Did you claim tax credits and a grant in the same year?
<--- Score

41. What software is eligible?
<--- Score

42. What is the benefit of the R&D credit?
<--- Score

43. What are transferable credits?
<--- Score

44. Who will determine interim and final deadlines?
<--- Score

45. What purposes did you have in undertaking the experimental activities?
<--- Score

46. Do you expect to have tax liability this year or coming years?
<--- Score

47. How does your state compare to other states?
<--- Score

48. Are the tax credit programs providing benefits to the intended customer?
<--- Score

49. What does available evidence say about the stimulative effect of the credit?
<--- Score

50. What are the consequences of not conducting the research?
<--- Score

51. How do you maximize your R&D Tax Credit?
<--- Score

52. What types of expenditure can you claim a tax offset for?
<--- Score

53. Applicable to existing IP?
<--- Score

54. Is the expenditure or loss for another person to perform R&D activities on behalf of the person?
<--- Score

55. How do you claim the R&D Credit?
<--- Score

56. What R&D activities are eligible?
<--- Score

57. Tax incentives and direct support for R&D: what does your organization use and why?
<--- Score

58. When are activities associated with compliance?
<--- Score

59. If you do not conduct R&D outside your country, why not?
<--- Score

60. What types of expenditure can companies claim a tax offset for?
<--- Score

61. Do subsidies to commercial R&D reduce market failures?
<--- Score

62. What are the policy and procedural implications?
<--- Score

63. How much credit does a business receive?
<--- Score

64. What affects how often you conduct R&D?
<--- Score

65. What is the tax period?
<--- Score

66. What proportion of R&D performed is your research?
<--- Score

67. What kinds of companies should investigate the R&D credit?
<--- Score

68. Do R&D tax credits increase the proportion of organizations that perform R&D?
<--- Score

69. What are the advantages?
<--- Score

70. What is a start-up organization for R&D Credit purposes?
<--- Score

71. Do R&D tax incentives stimulate the entry of new innovative firms?
<--- Score

72. Do you feel that more should be done in the Research and Development Tax Credit area?
<--- Score

73. How and when do you apply?
<--- Score

74. What platforms do you use?
<--- Score

75. Do R&D subsidies increase the level of R&D expenditure by subsidized firms?

<--- Score

76. How will a recession change your picture?

<--- Score

77. What is an unauthorized commitment?

<--- Score

78. How long will it take to change?

<--- Score

79. What could happen if you do not do it?

<--- Score

80. Of the total, how much was paid to a tax agent or other consultant?

<--- Score

81. What motivated you to apply?

<--- Score

82. What activities are eligible?

<--- Score

83. How much R&D do you do in your country?

<--- Score

84. Have you registered your activities?

<--- Score

85. What is the benefit of performing R&D?

<--- Score

86. Do you hold patents/IP?
<--- Score

87. What are your concerns?
<--- Score

88. Can you use estimates?
<--- Score

89. If you were responsible for initiating and implementing major changes in your organization, what steps might you take to ensure acceptance of those changes?
<--- Score

90. If you find that you havent accomplished one of the goals for one of the steps of the Research and Development Tax Credit strategy, what will you do to fix it?
<--- Score

91. Did you conduct R&D prior to YEAR (either in or outside your country)?
<--- Score

92. Are resources available in house?
<--- Score

93. Does money really matter?
<--- Score

94. How effective are additional tax credits for R&D?
<--- Score

95. What factors should you take into account

when deciding how centralized your R&D activities should be?
<--- Score

96. Are you / should you be revolutionary or evolutionary?
<--- Score

97. How is the Credit Calculated?
<--- Score

98. Which test is appropriate?
<--- Score

99. Tax incentives or subsidies for R&D?
<--- Score

100. Are you maintaining a past–present–future perspective throughout the Research and Development Tax Credit discussion?
<--- Score

101. Does your organization have a formal code of conduct?
<--- Score

102. What about other incentives?
<--- Score

103. Why is the tension between centralization and decentralization of R&D activities likely to be even greater for multinational organizations than organizations that compete in one national market?
<--- Score

104. Who is likely to have an interest in the topic?
<--- Score

105. How does charitable giving respond to incentives and income?
<--- Score

106. Are the activities or projects technical in nature?
<--- Score

107. What happens if projects are fee paid - what does subsidised mean?
<--- Score

108. What is it that you intend to communicate to others?
<--- Score

109. What kinds of business income do you have to report on your tax return?
<--- Score

110. What are the barriers to increased Research and Development Tax Credit production?
<--- Score

111. Have you applied for other grants, subsidies or tax credits before?
<--- Score

112. How effective are R&D incentives?
<--- Score

113. Have you conducted any R&D since YEAR?
<--- Score

114. What if you do not have enough tax liability to use all of the credit?
<--- Score

115. Is the research technological in nature?
<--- Score

116. How do you determine the amount of credits allowable to each entity?
<--- Score

117. Are there systems of support and protection in place for disclosers?
<--- Score

118. What kinds of people are most creative?
<--- Score

119. Are R&D tax credits effective?
<--- Score

120. Why pursue the R&D Credit?
<--- Score

121. Are you liable to Corporation Tax?
<--- Score

122. Is your capital gain or loss short term or long term?
<--- Score

123. Why should you offer it?
<--- Score

124. How much credit is allowed?

<--- Score

125. R&D tax credit revenue audit readiness: how strong is your endgame?
<--- Score

126. What must you attach?
<--- Score

127. What is new knowledge?
<--- Score

128. What you are seeing as current trends?
<--- Score

129. What considerations did you have about it before applying?
<--- Score

130. Do tax credits stimulate R&D spending?
<--- Score

131. How do you claim the R&D Tax Credit?
<--- Score

132. What are your most important goals for the strategic Research and Development Tax Credit objectives?
<--- Score

133. Did you aim to get as many points as possible, or just enough to pass?
<--- Score

134. How do you know if you can claim the R&D Tax Credits?

<--- Score

135. Can you carry unused credit to future tax years?
<--- Score

136. How would it work for a small organization that is not a startup?
<--- Score

137. What is the average period of a R&D project from initiation to commercial success?
<--- Score

138. How is the credit utilized?
<--- Score

139. What about local business tax expenditures?
<--- Score

140. Operational - will it work?
<--- Score

141. Why was the R&D tax credit created?
<--- Score

142. What happens when a new employee joins the organization?
<--- Score

143. Is R&D sensitive to cyclical changes and thus important to catch on a quarterly basis?
<--- Score

144. Who should consider purchasing transferable credits?

<--- Score

145. Who do you think the world wants your organization to be?
<--- Score

146. How much can you expect to get back?
<--- Score

147. Who has a vested interest in the status quo?
<--- Score

148. What are the communication methods to use?
<--- Score

149. Corporate tax disclosure: good or bad for your organization?
<--- Score

150. What return do they look for?
<--- Score

151. How do you make it meaningful in connecting Research and Development Tax Credit with what users do day-to-day?
<--- Score

152. Who should consider selling transferable credits?
<--- Score

153. Is the R&D technological in nature?
<--- Score

154. Who are the R&D Activities conducted for?
<--- Score

155. Who runs the program?

<--- Score

156. What is the scientific or technological advance?

<--- Score

157. What kinds of R&D tax incentives are being used?

<--- Score

158. Do equity financing cycles matter?

<--- Score

159. Which companies does it apply to?

<--- Score

160. Must third-party research be performed within an enterprise zone?

<--- Score

161. How does the acquisition or disposition of a business entity affect the R&D Credit computation?

<--- Score

162. How important is Research and Development Tax Credit to the user organizations mission?

<--- Score

163. Who have you, as a company, historically been when you've been at your best?

<--- Score

164. Why do governments have policies that

stimulate innovation?

<--- Score

165. How is your organization structured?

<--- Score

166. How effective are level-based R&D tax credits ?

<--- Score

167. What are basic research payments for R&D Credit?

<--- Score

168. How big are major projects?

<--- Score

169. Will it work?

<--- Score

170. What would have to be true for the option on the table to be the best possible choice?

<--- Score

171. Can support from partners be adjusted?

<--- Score

172. How long will it take to receive an R&D tax credit repayment?

<--- Score

173. Do you use Trainees/Apprentices?

<--- Score

174. Does the area of research fall within a social science, the arts or humanities?

<--- Score

175. What would happen without the credit?
<--- Score

176. Where does energy R&D come from?
<--- Score

177. Does your organization have a project?
<--- Score

178. What will be the consequences to the stakeholder (financial, reputation etc) if Research and Development Tax Credit does not go ahead or fails to deliver the objectives?
<--- Score

179. What are the eligibility criteria?
<--- Score

180. How important is R&D for economic growth?
<--- Score

181. Does your organization have linked or partner companies?
<--- Score

182. Is Research and Development Tax Credit realistic, or are you setting yourself up for failure?
<--- Score

183. How easy/difficult is it to claim tax credits/ grants?
<--- Score

184. Can you do it again?

<--- Score

185. What is the ideal situation?
<--- Score

186. Do you incorporate the tax credit/grant in the calculation of ROI?
<--- Score

187. R&D investment at your organization level: does the source of financing matter?
<--- Score

188. How effective are level-based R&D tax credits?
<--- Score

189. Do you use Graduates/PhDs?
<--- Score

190. Have you undertaken eligible R&D activities?
<--- Score

191. What would your organization have realized if they had not received the treatment?
<--- Score

192. Why does the date of introduction matter?
<--- Score

193. How is the credit computed?
<--- Score

194. Are any significant changes expected over the coming months?
<--- Score

195. Is an alternative simplified credit on your organizations research spending?
<--- Score

196. What does research include?
<--- Score

197. Do your leaders quickly bounce back from setbacks?
<--- Score

198. Can you write it off?
<--- Score

199. Has your program been audited?
<--- Score

200. Research and experimentation tax credits: who got how much?
<--- Score

201. Do state and local tax incentives work?
<--- Score

202. Are you eligible for R&D credits?
<--- Score

203. What records should be maintained?
<--- Score

204. Was your hypothesis testable (i.e. could it be proven or disproven)?
<--- Score

205. Do you have a claim?

<--- Score

206. What are your personal philosophies regarding Research and Development Tax Credit and how do they influence your work?
<--- Score

207. What outcomes are expected?
<--- Score

208. Is the credit refundable or nonrefundable?
<--- Score

209. Do you use Test Facilities?
<--- Score

210. What work is eligible?
<--- Score

211. Does your organization provide feedback and rewards for good work?
<--- Score

212. Does an R&D tax credit affect R&D expenditure?
<--- Score

213. Why do governments support business R&D?
<--- Score

214. Is your basic point _____ or _____?
<--- Score

215. How much basic research is desirable in what kind of an R&D lab?
<--- Score

216. How soon do you want to implement it?
<--- Score

217. Are you an eligible R&D entity?
<--- Score

218. Is the program meeting acceptable criteria for state investment?
<--- Score

219. Have any significant changes occurred in your organization over the past few months?
<--- Score

220. Is the R&D tax credit effective?
<--- Score

221. Would this be an advance in the knowledge to the general market place?
<--- Score

222. What is the policy rationale for the research credit?
<--- Score

223. How is it different from before?
<--- Score

224. To what degree is there a market pull?
<--- Score

225. Do R&D tax credits work?
<--- Score

226. Which companies are eligible?

<--- Score

227. Where do you move on, where do you stop?
<--- Score

228. How do you know if your activities are eligible?
<--- Score

229. Should the government promote R&D?
<--- Score

230. Does your company perform research?
<--- Score

231. Who is on the team?
<--- Score

232. Do R&D subsidies stimulate or displace private R&D?
<--- Score

233. Is public R&D a complement or substitute for private R&D?
<--- Score

234. Who is eligible to compute and claim the credit?
<--- Score

235. Do you think this is something that would benefit smaller businesses?
<--- Score

236. Can an R&D tax credit be properly designed for economic efficiency?

<--- Score

237. How do you create buy-in?
<--- Score

238. How does the inclusion of a partnership affect the R&D Credit?
<--- Score

239. How do you access the program?
<--- Score

240. What does a claimant do if it cannot demonstrate that it conducted a comprehensive literature review at the outset of the project?
<--- Score

241. What kinds of sources are most effective?
<--- Score

242. Who is eligible to compute the credit?
<--- Score

243. Which benefits should you offer?
<--- Score

244. What barriers do you continue to face?
<--- Score

245. How much does the credit reduce tax revenues?
<--- Score

246. Which forms must you file?
<--- Score

247. Do the effects of R&D tax credits vary across industries?

<--- Score

248. How often do tax audits take place?

<--- Score

249. Does your state conform to federal R&D credit provisions?

<--- Score

250. What should a code of conduct contain?

<--- Score

251. Did you conduct an experiment?

<--- Score

252. If your organization was to receive new/more tax relief on R&D expenditure, will this all be re-invested in extra R&D in the future?

<--- Score

253. Who is the main stakeholder, with ultimate responsibility for driving Research and Development Tax Credit forward?

<--- Score

254. What evidence do you have to support your claim?

<--- Score

255. What does the future hold?

<--- Score

256. Is there a provision for return of your organizations investment if certain criteria are not

met?

<--- Score

257. Public funding of child-care services: subsidy or human capital investment?

<--- Score

258. Is the persons R&D tax credit more than the persons outstanding tax liability?

<--- Score

259. Why is the R&D tax credit relevant to your organization now?

<--- Score

260. If you promise to build it, will they come?

<--- Score

261. What is eligible R&D?

<--- Score

262. Does it work in the intended way?

<--- Score

263. Does your organization have a hotline for reporting concerns?

<--- Score

264. Who do you want your customers to become?

<--- Score

265. Who is eligible to claim the credit?

<--- Score

266. Have you carried out eligible activities?

<--- Score

267. Who is eligible for the Credit?

<--- Score

268. How is the R&D tax credit calculated?

<--- Score

269. Which investments are eligible for the relief?

<--- Score

270. For supporting activities, why were they integral to the core activity?

<--- Score

271. How effective are fiscal incentives for R&D?

<--- Score

272. How much of your refund is left?

<--- Score

273. Is the credit incremental?

<--- Score

274. What happens if you have a business loss?

<--- Score

275. How do you calculate the credit?

<--- Score

276. For whom are the R&D activities conducted?

<--- Score

277. What are the core benefits of the R&D credit?

<--- Score

278. What systematic approach was used to

conduct the activity?
<--- Score

279. What is the overall business strategy?
<--- Score

280. How effective are fiscal incentives for R & D?
<--- Score

281. When can the credit be claimed?
<--- Score

282. How often do you conduct R&D?
<--- Score

283. What is the typical timeframe of R&D investment?
<--- Score

284. Where can you turn when looking to fund activities and projects that could contribute to growth?
<--- Score

285. Does it fit the Road Map?
<--- Score

286. Is the credit refundable?
<--- Score

287. Will you be incentivised to undertake more R&D by the tax credit?
<--- Score

288. In what years can you claim the credit?
<--- Score

289. Do you write and/or adapt software?

<--- Score

290. Will pursuing the credit pay off for your organization?

<--- Score

291. Do you consider Intellectual Property to be of strategic value to the business?

<--- Score

292. Do other countries offer similar R&D tax incentives?

<--- Score

293. Can the credit reduce alternative minimum tax?

<--- Score

294. How are transactions between head office and branch treated?

<--- Score

295. How can the R&D credit benefit you?

<--- Score

296. Is funding adequate?

<--- Score

297. How efficient is the programme?

<--- Score

298. How do you transition from the baseline to the target?

<--- Score

299. Why would you do R&D?
<--- Score

300. How is implementation research currently incorporated into each of your goals?
<--- Score

301. How much is the credit?
<--- Score

302. On what schedule and form do you claim the credit?
<--- Score

303. What is holding the industry back from making R&D tax credit claims?
<--- Score

304. How far can you go back to claim?
<--- Score

305. To what degree can the innovation be tried on a limited basis?
<--- Score

306. When can the taxpayer claim the credit?
<--- Score

307. Is there a work around that you can use?
<--- Score

308. Do you use subcontractors?
<--- Score

309. How do you apply?

<--- Score

310. Is R&D financially constrained?
<--- Score

311. Have you checked that your activity is not excluded from being a core R&D activity?
<--- Score

312. What if your credit is more than the taxes you owe?
<--- Score

313. Did your experiment investigate and test a hypothesis?
<--- Score

314. What must you excel at?
<--- Score

315. Are there audits done electronically in your country (e-audit)?
<--- Score

316. What credit is available?
<--- Score

317. How much has been invested?
<--- Score

318. Do you have the people who are able to conduct basic research?
<--- Score

319. Is the expenditure or loss incurred on a R&D activity for an income year?

<--- Score

320. Has the person filed tax return and R&D supplementary return by the deadline?
<--- Score

321. Are the overall resource allocations for R&D investments appropriate?
<--- Score

322. What does it offer?
<--- Score

323. Who is responsible for ensuring appropriate resources (time, people and money) are allocated to Research and Development Tax Credit?
<--- Score

324. Have you undertaken supporting R&D activities?
<--- Score

325. Does the activity involve research (whether it includes an experiment or not)?
<--- Score

326. How can you incorporate support to ensure safe and effective use of Research and Development Tax Credit into the services that you provide?
<--- Score

327. Is a value added tax progressive?
<--- Score

328. Are R&D tax credits desirable?
<--- Score

329. What unique value proposition (UVP) do you offer?
<--- Score

330. What is new in the R&D tax credit area?
<--- Score

331. How do you catch Research and Development Tax Credit definition inconsistencies?
<--- Score

332. Do they have specialist/dedicated R&D resources?
<--- Score

333. What are the short and long-term Research and Development Tax Credit goals?
<--- Score

334. How much credit does your business receive?
<--- Score

335. Is it a changing tax for changing times?
<--- Score

336. What forms must you file?
<--- Score

337. How do you figure a gain or loss?
<--- Score

338. Was one of corresponding purposes to generate new knowledge?
<--- Score

339. Is your practice liable to corporation tax?
<--- Score

340. Why is it important to have senior management support for a Research and Development Tax Credit project?
<--- Score

341. How do corresponding credits make mergers and acquisitions more attractive?
<--- Score

342. Who is not eligible to apply?
<--- Score

343. Are the criteria for selecting recommendations stated?
<--- Score

344. What records should your organization keep?
<--- Score

345. What has changed in recent years?
<--- Score

346. Why do you conduct R&D?
<--- Score

347. Why do and why don't your customers like your organization?
<--- Score

348. How effective is the R&D tax credit?
<--- Score

349. What type(s) of research is your company

undertaking?

<--- Score

350. What types of projects are eligible?

<--- Score

351. What does it take for an R&D tax incentive policy to be effective?

<--- Score

352. In a project to restructure Research and Development Tax Credit outcomes, which stakeholders would you involve?

<--- Score

353. Can you share the credit with other members?

<--- Score

354. How would you describe your business model?

<--- Score

355. How much is the R&D tax credit scheme worth?

<--- Score

356. How much is it worth?

<--- Score

357. Do you have the right capabilities and capacities?

<--- Score

358. Which functions and people interact with the supplier and or customer?

<--- Score

359. Are there consequences of not conducting the research?

<--- Score

360. What is your competitive advantage?

<--- Score

361. Is a person eligible for the R&D tax credit?

<--- Score

362. What is the difference between a tax incentive and a tax credit?

<--- Score

363. Does it move the product towards its next evolution?

<--- Score

364. What may be the consequences for the performance of an organization if all stakeholders are not consulted regarding Research and Development Tax Credit?

<--- Score

365. What have been your experiences in defining long range Research and Development Tax Credit goals?

<--- Score

366. How would a small organization claim an R&D tax credit?

<--- Score

367. Are there reasons why continuity rules should not apply to tax credits?

<--- Score

368. How do you promote it?
<--- Score

369. How do you calculate the credit amount?
<--- Score

370. What must you do if you have employees?
<--- Score

371. Do you use Consultants?
<--- Score

372. Is maximizing Research and Development Tax Credit protection the same as minimizing Research and Development Tax Credit loss?
<--- Score

373. Do R&D tax incentives work?
<--- Score

374. Are substantial rights in research retained?
<--- Score

375. What are the key challenges for your organization now and over the next three to five years?
<--- Score

376. How do you treat R&D losses?
<--- Score

377. When must you claim the credit?
<--- Score

378. What are your payment options?

<--- Score

379. Is new research in this field necessary?
<--- Score

380. How will you tell if you have a significant purpose?
<--- Score

381. Is the activity an eligible R&D activity?
<--- Score

382. What is next for jobs and hiring?
<--- Score

383. Was the most significant purpose of undertaking the activity to support one or more core R&D activities?
<--- Score

384. What are the aggregation rules?
<--- Score

385. What events or activities can you use to help communicate with the target audiences?
<--- Score

386. Who participates in R&D subsidy programs?
<--- Score

387. How does R&D tax policy affect your R&D?
<--- Score

388. What are your responsibilities and entitlements?
<--- Score

389. Growth & return in relation with R&D expenses ?
<--- Score

390. How effective is the programme?
<--- Score

391. Do tax incentives affect investment?
<--- Score

392. What method do you use to account for your income and expenses?
<--- Score

393. Is the activity conducted using a systematic approach?
<--- Score

394. How important is a cap or a mechanism to go beyond the cap?
<--- Score

Add up total points for this section:
_ _ _ _ _ = Total points for this section

Divided by: _ _ _ _ _ _ (number of
statements answered) = _ _ _ _ _ _
Average score for this section

Transfer your score to the Research and Development Tax Credit Index at the beginning of the Self-Assessment.

Research And Development Tax Credit and Managing Projects, Criteria for Project Managers:

1.0 Initiating Process Group: Research And Development Tax Credit

1. Does it make any difference if you am successful?

2. At which stage, in a typical Research And Development Tax Credit project do stake holders have maximum influence?

3. Have requirements been tested, approved, and fulfill the Research And Development Tax Credit project scope?

4. If the risk event occurs, what will you do?

5. What are the required resources?

6. What are the short and long term implications?

7. Did you use a contractor or vendor?

8. Where must it be done?

9. What were things that you did very well and want to do the same again on the next Research And Development Tax Credit project?

10. What is the stake of others in your Research And Development Tax Credit project?

11. How will you do it?

12. How to control and approve each phase?

13. Do you understand the quality and control criteria

that must be achieved for successful Research And Development Tax Credit project completion?

14. During which stage of Risk planning are risks prioritized based on probability and impact?

15. Have you evaluated the teams performance and asked for feedback?

16. What are the tools and techniques to be used in each phase?

17. What are the constraints?

18. What were things that you need to improve?

19. Which six sigma dmaic phase focuses on why and how defects and errors occur?

20. Were resources available as planned?

1.1 Project Charter: Research And Development Tax Credit

21. Did your Research And Development Tax Credit project ask for this?

22. Strategic fit: what is the strategic initiative identifier for this Research And Development Tax Credit project?

23. What are the assumptions?

24. How will you know a change is an improvement?

25. What goes into your Research And Development Tax Credit project Charter?

26. When?

27. What are the deliverables?

28. Who ise input and support will this Research And Development Tax Credit project require?

29. What is the justification?

30. Major high-level milestone targets: what events measure progress?

31. Are you building in-house ?

32. Research And Development Tax Credit project deliverables: what is the Research And Development

Tax Credit project going to produce?

33. Market – identify products market, including whether it is outside of the objective: what is the purpose of the program or Research And Development Tax Credit project?

34. What ideas do you have for initial tests of change (PDSA cycles)?

35. Why is a Research And Development Tax Credit project Charter used?

36. Dependent Research And Development Tax Credit projects: what Research And Development Tax Credit projects must be underway or completed before this Research And Development Tax Credit project can be successful?

37. Assumptions and constraints: what assumptions were made in defining the Research And Development Tax Credit project?

38. What date will the task finish?

39. What are the known stakeholder requirements?

40. Avoid costs, improve service, and/ or comply with a mandate?

1.2 Stakeholder Register: Research And Development Tax Credit

41. Who are the stakeholders?

42. Who wants to talk about Security?

43. What & Why?

44. How much influence do they have on the Research And Development Tax Credit project?

45. How big is the gap?

46. What is the power of the stakeholder?

47. How will reports be created?

48. What are the major Research And Development Tax Credit project milestones requiring communications or providing communications opportunities?

49. What opportunities exist to provide communications?

50. Who is managing stakeholder engagement?

51. How should employers make voices heard?

52. Is your organization ready for change?

1.3 Stakeholder Analysis Matrix: Research And Development Tax Credit

53. Why do you care?

54. How are the threatened Research And Development Tax Credit project targets being used?

55. What tools would help you communicate?

56. Alliances: with which other actors is the actor allied, how are they interconnected?

57. Who determines value?

58. What do people from other organizations see as your organizations weaknesses?

59. What are the mechanisms of public and social accountability, and how can they be made better?

60. Who will be responsible for managing the outcome?

61. Gaps in capabilities?

62. Which conditions out of the control of the management are crucial for the achievement of the outputs?

63. Usps (unique selling points)?

64. How will the stakeholder directly benefit from the

Research And Development Tax Credit project and how will this affect the stakeholders motivation?

65. How can you counter negative efforts?

66. Own known vulnerabilities?

67. Guiding question: what is the issue at stake?

68. Why involve the stakeholder?

69. How to measure the achievement of the Immediate Objective?

70. What do people from other organizations see as your strengths?

71. Effects on core activities, distraction?

72. What can the stakeholder prevent from happening?

2.0 Planning Process Group: Research And Development Tax Credit

73. What business situation is being addressed?

74. How can you make your needs known?

75. Product breakdown structure (pbs): what is the Research And Development Tax Credit project result or product, and how should it look like, what are its parts?

76. Why do it Research And Development Tax Credit projects fail?

77. What is the critical path for this Research And Development Tax Credit project, and what is the duration of the critical path?

78. If a task is partitionable, is this a sufficient condition to reduce the Research And Development Tax Credit project duration?

79. Mitigate. what will you do to minimize the impact should a risk event occur?

80. How are the principles of aid effectiveness (ownership, alignment, management for development results and mutual responsibility) being applied in the Research And Development Tax Credit project?

81. How do you integrate Research And Development

Tax Credit project Planning with the Iterative/
Evolutionary SDLC?

82. How can you tell when you are done?

83. What type of estimation method are you using?

84. Professionals want to know what is expected from
them; what are the deliverables?

85. How will it affect you?

86. To what extent has a PMO contributed to raising
the quality of the design of the Research And
Development Tax Credit project?

87. What is the difference between the early schedule
and late schedule?

88. To what extent are the visions and actions of the
partners consistent or divergent with regard to the
program?

89. Contingency planning. if a risk event occurs, what
will you do?

90. Is the Research And Development Tax Credit
project supported by national and/or local
organizations?

91. Is the schedule for the set products being met?

92. Why is it important to determine activity
sequencing on Research And Development Tax Credit
projects?

2.1 Project Management Plan: Research And Development Tax Credit

93. What is risk management?

94. Is the engineering content at a feasibility level-of-detail, and is it sufficiently complete, to provide an adequate basis for the baseline cost estimate?

95. What is the business need?

96. Will you add a schedule and diagram?

97. What data/reports/tools/etc. do your PMs need?

98. How do you manage integration?

99. Did the planning effort collaborate to develop solutions that integrate expertise, policies, programs, and Research And Development Tax Credit projects across entities?

100. Are calculations and results of analyzes essentially correct?

101. What would you do differently what did not work?

102. Why do you manage integration?

103. Are there any scope changes proposed for a previously authorized Research And Development Tax Credit project?

104. Do the proposed changes from the Research And Development Tax Credit project include any significant risks to safety?

105. If the Research And Development Tax Credit project is complex or scope is specialized, do you have appropriate and/or qualified staff available to perform the tasks?

106. How well are you able to manage your risk?

107. Is mitigation authorized or recommended?

108. How do you manage time?

109. Is the budget realistic?

110. What would you do differently?

2.2 Scope Management Plan: Research And Development Tax Credit

111. Has a provision been made to reassess Research And Development Tax Credit project risks at various Research And Development Tax Credit project stages?

112. How many changes are you making?

113. Do you have funding for Research And Development Tax Credit project and product development, implementation and on-going support?

114. Can the Research And Development Tax Credit project team do several activities in parallel?

115. Are Research And Development Tax Credit project leaders committed to this Research And Development Tax Credit project full time?

116. When will scope verification be performed?

117. Pareto diagrams, statistical sampling, flow charting or trend analysis used quality monitoring?

118. Has allowance been made for vacations, holidays, training (learning time for each team member), staff promotions & staff turnovers?

119. Has appropriate allowance been made for the effect of the learning curve on all personnel joining the Research And Development Tax Credit

project who do not have the required prior industry, functional & technical expertise?

120. Quality standards - are controls in place to ensure that the work was not only completed and also completed to meet specific standards?

121. What are the risks that could significantly affect the communication on the Research And Development Tax Credit project?

122. What is the unique product, service or result?

123. Was the scope definition used in task sequencing?

124. Will anyone else be involved in verifying the deliverables?

125. Is the quality assurance team identified?

126. Has a proper Research And Development Tax Credit project work location been established that will allow the team to work together with user personnel?

127. Have the scope, objectives, costs, benefits and impacts been communicated to all involved and/or impacted stakeholders and work groups?

128. What happens if scope changes?

129. What happens to rejected deliverables?

130. What weaknesses do you have?

2.3 Requirements Management Plan: Research And Development Tax Credit

131. Why manage requirements?

132. What are you counting on?

133. Did you provide clear and concise specifications?

134. Does the Research And Development Tax Credit project have a Change Control process?

135. Is requirements work dependent on any other specific Research And Development Tax Credit project or non-Research And Development Tax Credit project activities (e.g. funding, approvals, procurement)?

136. How will the requirements become prioritized?

137. Who is responsible for monitoring and tracking the Research And Development Tax Credit project requirements?

138. Will you document changes to requirements?

139. Is infrastructure setup part of your Research And Development Tax Credit project?

140. How often will the reporting occur?

141. Who will perform the analysis?

142. Are actual resources expenditures versus planned

expenditures acceptable?

143. Who will approve the requirements (and if multiple approvers, in what order)?

144. Who has the authority to reject Research And Development Tax Credit project requirements?

145. How will unresolved questions be handled once approval has been obtained?

146. How will you develop the schedule of requirements activities?

147. Do you have an appropriate arrangement for meetings?

148. How detailed should the Research And Development Tax Credit project get?

149. Do you have price sheets and a methodology for determining the total proposal cost?

150. Did you use declarative statements?

2.4 Requirements Documentation: Research And Development Tax Credit

151. How linear / iterative is your Requirements Gathering process (or will it be)?

152. What are current process problems?

153. What are the acceptance criteria?

154. Does the system provide the functions which best support the customers needs?

155. Is your business case still valid?

156. Has requirements gathering uncovered information that would necessitate changes?

157. Can you check system requirements?

158. What will be the integration problems?

159. Is the requirement realistically testable?

160. How will they be documented / shared?

161. How can you document system requirements?

162. What is the risk associated with the technology?

163. What kind of entity is a problem ?

164. The problem with gathering requirements is

right there in the word gathering. What images does it conjure?

165. What is your Elevator Speech?

166. Are there legal issues?

167. Are all functions required by the customer included?

168. What are the attributes of a customer?

169. Is the origin of the requirement clearly stated?

170. How does what is being described meet the business need?

2.5 Requirements Traceability Matrix: Research And Development Tax Credit

171. How small is small enough?

172. Do you have a clear understanding of all subcontracts in place?

173. Will you use a Requirements Traceability Matrix?

174. What percentage of Research And Development Tax Credit projects are producing traceability matrices between requirements and other work products?

175. How do you manage scope?

176. What are the chronologies, contingencies, consequences, criteria?

177. Why use a WBS?

178. How will it affect the stakeholders personally in career?

179. Why do you manage scope?

180. What is the WBS?

181. Describe the process for approving requirements so they can be added to the traceability matrix and Research And Development Tax Credit project work can be performed. Will the Research And Development Tax Credit project requirements

become approved in writing?

182. Is there a requirements traceability process in place?

2.6 Project Scope Statement: Research And Development Tax Credit

183. Write a brief purpose statement for this Research And Development Tax Credit project. Include a business justification statement. What is the product of this Research And Development Tax Credit project?

184. Elements of scope management that deal with concept development ?

185. Elements that deal with providing the detail?

186. Change management vs. change leadership - what is the difference?

187. Is the scope of your Research And Development Tax Credit project well defined?

188. Are the meetings set up to have assigned note takers that will add action/issues to the issue list?

189. Research And Development Tax Credit project lead, team lead, solution architect?

190. Have you been able to easily identify success criteria and create objective measurements for each of the Research And Development Tax Credit project scopes goal statements?

191. If there is an independent oversight contractor, have they signed off on the Research And Development Tax Credit project Plan?

192. Will the Research And Development Tax Credit project risks be managed according to the Research And Development Tax Credit projects risk management process?

193. Has the format for tracking and monitoring schedules and costs been defined?

194. Any new risks introduced or old risks impacted. Are there issues that could affect the existing requirements for the result, service, or product if the scope changes?

195. Will all Research And Development Tax Credit project issues be unconditionally tracked through the issue resolution process?

196. What is change?

197. Will tasks be marked complete only after QA has been successfully completed?

198. Were key Research And Development Tax Credit project stakeholders brought into the Research And Development Tax Credit project Plan?

199. Will you need a statement of work?

200. Is there a Change Management Board?

201. What are the defined meeting materials?

202. What went right?

2.7 Assumption and Constraint Log: Research And Development Tax Credit

203. What would you gain if you spent time working to improve this process?

204. Does the system design reflect the requirements?

205. Has the approach and development strategy of the Research And Development Tax Credit project been defined, documented and accepted by the appropriate stakeholders?

206. What strengths do you have?

207. Are there nonconformance issues?

208. Are formal code reviews conducted?

209. What do you audit?

210. Are funding and staffing resource estimates sufficiently detailed and documented for use in planning and tracking the Research And Development Tax Credit project?

211. How relevant is this attribute to this Research And Development Tax Credit project or audit?

212. Have adequate resources been provided by management to ensure Research And Development Tax Credit project success?

213. Are there processes in place to ensure that all the terms and code concepts have been documented consistently?

214. When can log be discarded?

215. No superfluous information or marketing narrative?

216. What threats might prevent you from getting there?

217. What if failure during recovery?

218. Does the plan conform to standards?

219. Are requirements management tracking tools and procedures in place?

220. Does the traceability documentation describe the tool and/or mechanism to be used to capture traceability throughout the life cycle?

221. Should factors be unpredictable over time?

2.8 Work Breakdown Structure: Research And Development Tax Credit

222. Why is it useful?

223. Is it still viable?

224. Who has to do it?

225. When do you stop?

226. How much detail?

227. How will you and your Research And Development Tax Credit project team define the Research And Development Tax Credit projects scope and work breakdown structure?

228. How far down?

229. How big is a work-package?

230. What has to be done?

231. Is it a change in scope?

232. Where does it take place?

233. Is the work breakdown structure (wbs) defined and is the scope of the Research And Development Tax Credit project clear with assigned deliverable owners?

234. Do you need another level?

235. How many levels?

236. Why would you develop a Work Breakdown Structure?

237. When does it have to be done?

238. What is the probability that the Research And Development Tax Credit project duration will exceed xx weeks?

239. Can you make it?

2.9 WBS Dictionary: Research And Development Tax Credit

240. Is data disseminated to the contractors management timely, accurate, and usable?

241. What should you drop in order to add something new?

242. Are procedures in existence that control replanning of unopened work packages, and are corresponding procedures adhered to?

243. Are authorized changes being incorporated in a timely manner?

244. Should you include sub-activities?

245. Cwbs elements to be subcontracted, with identification of subcontractors?

246. Contractor financial periods; for example, annual?

247. Are budgets or values assigned to work packages and planning packages in terms of dollars, hours, or other measurable units?

248. Budgets assigned to major functional organizations?

249. Do procedures specify under what circumstances replanning of open work packages may occur, and the

methods to be followed?

250. Are records maintained to show full accountability for all material purchased for the contract, including the residual inventory?

251. What is the end result of a work package?

252. Intermediate schedules, as required, which provide a logical sequence from the master schedule to the control account level?

253. Is authorization of budgets in excess of the contract budget base controlled formally and done with the full knowledge and recognition of the procuring activity?

254. Are the variances between budgeted and actual indirect costs identified and analyzed at the level of assigned responsibility for control (indirect pool, department, etc.)?

255. Is undistributed budget limited to contract effort which cannot yet be planned to CWBS elements at or below the level specified for reporting to the Government?

256. Is budgeted cost for work performed calculated in a manner consistent with the way work is planned?

257. Does the sum of all work package budgets plus planning packages within control accounts equal the budgets assigned to the already stated control accounts?

258. Appropriate work authorization documents

which subdivide the contractual effort and responsibilities, within functional organizations?

2.10 Schedule Management Plan: Research And Development Tax Credit

259. Does the ims include all contract and/or designated management control milestones?

260. Are issues raised, assessed, actioned, and resolved in a timely and efficient manner?

261. Will rolling way planning be used?

262. Is there a procedure for management, control and release of schedule margin?

263. Is Research And Development Tax Credit project status reviewed with the steering and executive teams at appropriate intervals?

264. Are non-critical path items updated and agreed upon with the teams?

265. Is there general agreement & acceptance of the current status and progress of the Research And Development Tax Credit project?

266. Does the time Research And Development Tax Credit projection include an amount for contingencies (time reserves)?

267. Does a documented Research And Development Tax Credit project organizational policy & plan (i.e. governance model) exist?

268. Has a provision been made to reassess Research And Development Tax Credit project risks at various Research And Development Tax Credit project stages?

269. Has a capability assessment been conducted?

270. Have the key functions and capabilities been defined and assigned to each release or iteration?

271. Have stakeholder accountabilities & responsibilities been clearly defined?

272. What is the difference between % Complete and % work?

273. Do Research And Development Tax Credit project teams & team members report on status / activities / progress?

274. Does the Research And Development Tax Credit project have a Quality Culture?

275. Have external dependencies been captured in the schedule?

276. List all schedule constraints here. Must the Research And Development Tax Credit project be complete by a specified date?

277. Are schedule performance measures defined including pre-set triggers for specific actions?

2.11 Activity List: Research And Development Tax Credit

278. What is your organizations history in doing similar activities?

279. How much slack is available in the Research And Development Tax Credit project?

280. How will it be performed?

281. What will be performed?

282. Are the required resources available or need to be acquired?

283. How can the Research And Development Tax Credit project be displayed graphically to better visualize the activities?

284. In what sequence?

285. When will the work be performed?

286. What are the critical bottleneck activities?

287. What went wrong?

288. Who will perform the work?

289. How difficult will it be to do specific activities on this Research And Development Tax Credit project?

290. What is the LF and LS for each activity?

291. What went well?

292. The wbs is developed as part of a joint planning session. and how do you know that youhave done this right?

293. How do you determine the late start (LS) for each activity?

294. What is the total time required to complete the Research And Development Tax Credit project if no delays occur?

295. How should ongoing costs be monitored to try to keep the Research And Development Tax Credit project within budget?

2.12 Activity Attributes: Research And Development Tax Credit

296. How difficult will it be to complete specific activities on this Research And Development Tax Credit project?

297. Is there anything planned that does not need to be here?

298. Can you re-assign any activities to another resource to resolve an over-allocation?

299. How difficult will it be to do specific activities on this Research And Development Tax Credit project?

300. Has management defined a definite timeframe for the turnaround or Research And Development Tax Credit project window?

301. Is there a trend during the year?

302. Do you feel very comfortable with your prediction?

303. What is missing?

304. What is the general pattern here?

305. Have you identified the Activity Leveling Priority code value on each activity?

306. How much activity detail is required?

307. Activity: what is Missing?

308. Activity: fair or not fair?

309. How many days do you need to complete the work scope with a limit of X number of resources?

310. How else could the items be grouped?

311. Are the required resources available?

312. Were there other ways you could have organized the data to achieve similar results?

2.13 Milestone List: Research And Development Tax Credit

313. Calculate how long can activity be delayed?

314. Describe your organizations strengths and core competencies. What factors will make your organization succeed?

315. Timescales, deadlines and pressures?

316. Insurmountable weaknesses?

317. How late can the activity finish?

318. What are your competitors vulnerabilities?

319. Can you derive how soon can the whole Research And Development Tax Credit project finish?

320. Level of the Innovation?

321. Vital contracts and partners?

322. How will the milestone be verified?

323. How late can each activity be finished and started?

324. How soon can the activity finish?

325. New USPs?

326. It is to be a narrative text providing the crucial aspects of your Research And Development Tax Credit project proposal answering what, who, how, when and where?

2.14 Network Diagram: Research And Development Tax Credit

327. What are the tools?

328. Where do you schedule uncertainty time?

329. What controls the start and finish of a job?

330. Where do schedules come from?

331. Are the gantt chart and/or network diagram updated periodically and used to assess the overall Research And Development Tax Credit project timetable?

332. What activity must be completed immediately before this activity can start?

333. Will crashing x weeks return more in benefits than it costs?

334. If x is long, what would be the completion time if you break x into two parallel parts of y weeks and z weeks?

335. What is the completion time?

336. What job or jobs precede it?

337. What to do and When?

338. What job or jobs could run concurrently?

339. What job or jobs follow it?

340. What is the lowest cost to complete this Research And Development Tax Credit project in xx weeks?

341. Can you calculate the confidence level?

342. If the Research And Development Tax Credit project network diagram cannot change and you have extra personnel resources, what is the BEST thing to do?

343. What activities must follow this activity?

344. Which type of network diagram allows you to depict four types of dependencies?

345. Review the logical flow of the network diagram. Take a look at which activities you have first and then sequence the activities. Do they make sense?

2.15 Activity Resource Requirements: Research And Development Tax Credit

346. Are there unresolved issues that need to be addressed?

347. When does monitoring begin?

348. Time for overtime?

349. How many signatures do you require on a check and does this match what is in your policy and procedures?

350. What is the Work Plan Standard?

351. Other support in specific areas?

352. Do you use tools like decomposition and rolling-wave planning to produce the activity list and other outputs?

353. Organizational Applicability?

354. Why do you do that?

355. What are constraints that you might find during the Human Resource Planning process?

356. Anything else?

357. Which logical relationship does the PDM use most often?

358. How do you handle petty cash?

2.16 Resource Breakdown Structure: Research And Development Tax Credit

359. What are the requirements for resource data?

360. Goals for the Research And Development Tax Credit project. What is each stakeholders desired outcome for the Research And Development Tax Credit project?

361. What is each stakeholders desired outcome for the Research And Development Tax Credit project?

362. Which resource planning tool provides information on resource responsibility and accountability?

363. Why is this important?

364. Is predictive resource analysis being done?

365. Changes based on input from stakeholders?

366. Who will use the system?

367. What is the number one predictor of a groups productivity?

368. Who is allowed to see what data about which resources?

369. Why do you do it?

370. The list could probably go on, but, the thing that you would most like to know is, How long & How much?

371. When do they need the information?

372. What is the primary purpose of the human resource plan?

373. Who delivers the information?

2.17 Activity Duration Estimates: Research And Development Tax Credit

374. Does a process exist to identify Research And Development Tax Credit project roles, responsibilities and reporting relationships?

375. Is the Research And Development Tax Credit project performing better or worse than planned?

376. Do procedures exist that identify when and how human resources are introduced and removed from the Research And Development Tax Credit project?

377. Will the new application negatively affect the current IT infrastructure?

378. Why should Research And Development Tax Credit project managers strive to make jobs look easy?

379. If you plan to take the PMP exam soon, what should you do to prepare?

380. What is the duration of a milestone?

381. Is training acquired to enhance the skills, knowledge and capabilities of the Research And Development Tax Credit project team?

382. Which is correct?

383. Are updates on work results collected and used

as inputs to the performance reporting process?

384. Are costs that may be needed to account for Research And Development Tax Credit project risks determined?

385. Which best describes the relationship between standard deviation and risk?

386. Is a contract developed which obligates the seller and the buyer?

387. Explanation notice how many choices are half right?

388. Consider the common sources of risk on information technology Research And Development Tax Credit projects and suggestions for managing them. Which suggestions do you find most useful?

389. Account for the make-or-buy process and how to perform the financial calculations involved in the process. What are the main types of contracts if you do decide to outsource?

390. Are expert judgment and historical information utilized to estimate activity duration?

391. Why is activity definition the first process involved in Research And Development Tax Credit project time management?

2.18 Duration Estimating Worksheet: Research And Development Tax Credit

392. What is the total time required to complete the Research And Development Tax Credit project if no delays occur?

393. Can the Research And Development Tax Credit project be constructed as planned?

394. What info is needed?

395. Why estimate time and cost?

396. When do the individual activities need to start and finish?

397. Does the Research And Development Tax Credit project provide innovative ways for stakeholders to overcome obstacles or deliver better outcomes?

398. What utility impacts are there?

399. Is this operation cost effective?

400. Will the Research And Development Tax Credit project collaborate with the local community and leverage resources?

401. What is your role?

402. Why estimate costs?

403. When, then?

404. What work will be included in the Research And Development Tax Credit project?

405. What is next?

406. For other activities, how much delay can be tolerated?

407. What is cost and Research And Development Tax Credit project cost management?

408. How should ongoing costs be monitored to try to keep the Research And Development Tax Credit project within budget?

2.19 Project Schedule: Research And Development Tax Credit

409. Is there a Schedule Management Plan that establishes the criteria and activities for developing, monitoring and controlling the Research And Development Tax Credit project schedule?

410. Master Research And Development Tax Credit project schedule?

411. How closely did the initial Research And Development Tax Credit project Schedule compare with the actual schedule?

412. Are there activities that came from a template or previous Research And Development Tax Credit project that are not applicable on this phase of this Research And Development Tax Credit project?

413. Are activities connected because logic dictates the order in which others occur?

414. What documents, if any, will the subcontractor provide (eg Research And Development Tax Credit project schedule, quality plan etc)?

415. How can you fix it?

416. How can you minimize or control changes to Research And Development Tax Credit project schedules?

417. Your Research And Development Tax Credit project management plan results in a Research And Development Tax Credit project schedule that is too long. If the Research And Development Tax Credit project network diagram cannot change and you have extra personnel resources, what is the BEST thing to do?

418. Activity charts and bar charts are graphical representations of a Research And Development Tax Credit project schedule ...how do they differ?

419. Is the structure for tracking the Research And Development Tax Credit project schedule well defined and assigned to a specific individual?

420. What is risk?

421. Eliminate unnecessary activities. Are there activities that came from a template or previous Research And Development Tax Credit project that are not applicable on this phase of this Research And Development Tax Credit project?

422. Why time management?

423. It allows the Research And Development Tax Credit project to be delivered on schedule. How Do you Use Schedules?

424. What is the most mis-scheduled part of process?

425. Why do you need schedules?

426. Is the Research And Development Tax Credit project schedule available for all Research And

Development Tax Credit project team members to review?

2.20 Cost Management Plan: Research And Development Tax Credit

427. Are risk oriented checklists used during risk identification?

428. Are there checklists created to determine if all quality processes are followed?

429. Have all unresolved risks been documented?

430. Time management – how will the schedule impact of changes be estimated and approved?

431. What would the life cycle costs be?

432. Milestones – what are the key dates in executing the contract plan?

433. Have process improvement efforts been completed before requirements efforts begin?

434. Is pert / critical path or equivalent methodology being used?

435. Is a payment system in place with proper reviews and approvals?

436. What is cost and Research And Development Tax Credit project cost management?

437. Are milestone deliverables effectively tracked and compared to Research And Development Tax

Credit project plan?

438. Are parking lot items captured?

439. What is your organizations history in doing similar tasks?

440. Are change requests logged and managed?

441. Has the schedule been baselined?

442. Have all involved Research And Development Tax Credit project stakeholders and work groups committed to the Research And Development Tax Credit project?

443. Is the structure for tracking the Research And Development Tax Credit project schedule well defined and assigned to a specific individual?

2.21 Activity Cost Estimates: Research And Development Tax Credit

444. Were sponsors and decision makers available when needed outside regularly scheduled meetings?

445. What are you looking for?

446. What areas does the group agree are the biggest success on the Research And Development Tax Credit project?

447. Padding is bad and contingencies are good. what is the difference?

448. Are data needed on characteristics of care?

449. What is the activity inventory?

450. What is included in indirect cost being allocated?

451. Which contract type places the most risk on the seller?

452. Where can you get activity reports?

453. What makes a good activity description?

454. What makes a good expected result statement?

455. Did the Research And Development Tax Credit project team have the right skills?

456. What is the activity recast of the budget?

457. Can you change your activities?

458. Were the tasks or work products prepared by the consultant useful?

459. Were the costs or charges reasonable?

460. Review – what are some common errors in activities to avoid?

461. Can you delete activities or make them inactive?

462. Who determines when the contractor is paid?

2.22 Cost Estimating Worksheet: Research And Development Tax Credit

463. What can be included?

464. What happens to any remaining funds not used?

465. Identify the timeframe necessary to monitor progress and collect data to determine how the selected measure has changed?

466. Will the Research And Development Tax Credit project collaborate with the local community and leverage resources?

467. Ask: are others positioned to know, are others credible, and will others cooperate?

468. What additional Research And Development Tax Credit project(s) could be initiated as a result of this Research And Development Tax Credit project?

469. Can a trend be established from historical performance data on the selected measure and are the criteria for using trend analysis or forecasting methods met?

470. Who is best positioned to know and assist in identifying corresponding factors?

471. Is it feasible to establish a control group arrangement?

472. Value pocket identification & quantification what are value pockets?

473. What is the purpose of estimating?

474. How will the results be shared and to whom?

475. Is the Research And Development Tax Credit project responsive to community need?

476. What is the estimated labor cost today based upon this information?

477. What will others want?

478. What costs are to be estimated?

479. Does the Research And Development Tax Credit project provide innovative ways for stakeholders to overcome obstacles or deliver better outcomes?

2.23 Cost Baseline: Research And Development Tax Credit

480. What can go wrong?

481. How do you manage cost?

482. Are procedures defined by which the cost baseline may be changed?

483. What deliverables come first?

484. Does the suggested change request seem to represent a necessary enhancement to the product?

485. Has the Research And Development Tax Credit project (or Research And Development Tax Credit project phase) been evaluated against each objective established in the product description and Integrated Research And Development Tax Credit project Plan?

486. Are you asking management for something as a result of this update?

487. How likely is it to go wrong?

488. Has the actual cost of the Research And Development Tax Credit project (or Research And Development Tax Credit project phase) been tallied and compared to the approved budget?

489. Definition of done can be traced back to the definitions of what are you providing to the customer

in terms of deliverables?

490. Is the cr within Research And Development Tax Credit project scope?

491. Who will use corresponding metrics ?

492. If you sold 10x widgets on a day, what would the affect on profits be?

493. Have all approved changes to the schedule baseline been identified and impact on the Research And Development Tax Credit project documented?

494. Have the resources used by the Research And Development Tax Credit project been reassigned to other units or Research And Development Tax Credit projects?

495. What do you want to measure ?

2.24 Quality Management Plan: Research And Development Tax Credit

496. Has a Research And Development Tax Credit project Communications Plan been developed?

497. Who is responsible?

498. How many Research And Development Tax Credit project staff does this specific process affect?

499. How effectively was the Quality Management Plan applied during Research And Development Tax Credit project Execution?

500. Are you meeting the quality standards?

501. Is there a Steering Committee in place?

502. How are changes to procedures made?

503. How do senior leaders create and communicate values and performance expectations?

504. Was trending evident between audits?

505. Is this a Requirement?

506. What type of in-house testing do you conduct?

507. What are your organizations key processes (product, service, business, and support)?

508. What worked well?

509. Have all stakeholders been identified?

510. Is the amount of effort justified by the anticipated value of forming a new process?

511. How does your organization decide what to measure?

512. Are there unnecessary steps that are creating bottlenecks and/or causing people to wait?

513. Can the requirements be traced to the appropriate components of the solution, as well as test scripts?

514. Are there processes in place to ensure internal consistency between the source code components?

2.25 Quality Metrics: Research And Development Tax Credit

515. Have risk areas been identified?

516. What metrics do you measure?

517. Is there a set of procedures to capture, analyze and act on quality metrics?

518. Should a modifier be included?

519. Subjective quality component: customer satisfaction, how do you measure it?

520. How do you calculate corresponding metrics?

521. Are quality metrics defined?

522. How should customers provide input?

523. How can the effectiveness of each of the activities be measured?

524. What is the timeline to meet your goal?

525. What does this tell us?

526. What metrics are important and most beneficial to measure?

527. Where did complaints, returns and warranty claims come from?

528. Have alternatives been defined in the event that failure occurs?

529. Can visual measures help you to filter visualizations of interest?

530. What is the CMS Benchmark?

531. What level of statistical confidence do you use?

532. Were quality attributes reported?

533. Did evaluation start on time?

2.26 Process Improvement Plan: Research And Development Tax Credit

534. What personnel are the change agents for your initiative?

535. Are you following the quality standards?

536. What is the test-cycle concept?

537. Are there forms and procedures to collect and record the data?

538. How do you manage quality?

539. What is quality and how will you ensure it?

540. How do you measure?

541. Have the frequency of collection and the points in the process where measurements will be made been determined?

542. Has the time line required to move measurement results from the points of collection to databases or users been established?

543. What personnel are the coaches for your initiative?

544. What personnel are the champions for the initiative?

545. Where do you want to be?

546. Does your process ensure quality?

547. Have storage and access mechanisms and procedures been determined?

548. The motive is determined by asking, Why do you want to achieve this goal?

549. What actions are needed to address the problems and achieve the goals?

550. Have the supporting tools been developed or acquired?

551. What is the return on investment?

2.27 Responsibility Assignment Matrix: Research And Development Tax Credit

552. Who is the sponsor?

553. Are overhead costs budgets established on a basis consistent with anticipated direct business base?

554. Is the entire contract planned in time-phased control accounts to the extent practicable?

555. Is the anticipated (firm and potential) business base Research And Development Tax Credit projected in a rational, consistent manner?

556. Which Research And Development Tax Credit project management knowledge area is least mature?

557. Are the requirements for all items of overhead established by rational, traceable processes?

558. Contract line items and end items?

559. Undistributed budgets, if any?

560. Are detailed work packages planned as far in advance as practicable?

561. Is every signing-off responsibility and every communicating responsibility critically necessary?

562. How do you assist them to be as productive as possible?

563. Contemplated overhead expenditure for each period based on the best information currently available?

564. Does the scheduling system identify in a timely manner the status of work?

565. Authorization to proceed with all authorized work?

566. Are all elements of indirect expense identified to overhead cost budgets of Research And Development Tax Credit projections?

567. Does the contractors system include procedures for measuring the performance of critical subcontractors?

568. What tool can show you individual and group allocations?

569. Are records maintained to show how undistributed budgets are controlled?

570. Does a missing responsibility indicate that the current Research And Development Tax Credit project is not yet fully understood?

571. Are material costs reported within the same period as that in which BCWP is earned for that material?

2.28 Roles and Responsibilities: Research And Development Tax Credit

572. What should you highlight for improvement?

573. Where are you most strong as a supervisor?

574. What is working well within your organizations performance management system?

575. What specific behaviors did you observe?

576. What should you do now to prepare yourself for a promotion, increased responsibilities or a different job?

577. Are Research And Development Tax Credit project team roles and responsibilities identified and documented?

578. Who is responsible for each task?

579. Was the expectation clearly communicated?

580. What are your major roles and responsibilities in the area of performance measurement and assessment?

581. What should you do now to ensure that you are meeting all expectations of your current position?

582. Concern: where are you limited or have no authority, where you can not influence?

583. Be specific; avoid generalities. Thank you and great work alone are insufficient. What exactly do you appreciate and why?

584. What areas would you highlight for changes or improvements?

585. Are Research And Development Tax Credit project team roles and responsibilities identified and documented?

586. Are governance roles and responsibilities documented?

587. Authority: what areas/Research And Development Tax Credit projects in your work do you have the authority to decide upon and act on the already stated decisions?

588. Are the quality assurance functions and related roles and responsibilities clearly defined?

589. Are your policies supportive of a culture of quality data?

590. What expectations were NOT met?

2.29 Human Resource Management Plan: Research And Development Tax Credit

591. Are enough systems & user personnel assigned to the Research And Development Tax Credit project?

592. Are quality inspections and review activities listed in the Research And Development Tax Credit project schedule(s)?

593. Specific - is the objective clear in terms of what, how, when, and where the situation will be changed?

594. Is your organization human?

595. What were things that you did very well and want to do the same again on the next Research And Development Tax Credit project?

596. Are Research And Development Tax Credit project leaders committed to this Research And Development Tax Credit project full time?

597. Is there a set of procedures defining the scope, procedures, and deliverables defining quality control?

598. Are the Research And Development Tax Credit project team members located locally to the users/ stakeholders?

599. Are changes in scope (deliverable commitments) agreed to by all affected groups & individuals?

600. Are the right people being attracted and retained to meet the future challenges?

601. Is there a Quality Management Plan?

602. Is there a formal set of procedures supporting Issues Management?

603. Who is involved?

604. Timeline and milestones?

605. How can below standard performers be guided/developed to upgrade performance?

2.30 Communications Management Plan: Research And Development Tax Credit

606. Which stakeholders are thought leaders, influences, or early adopters?

607. Do you feel a register helps?

608. Are stakeholders internal or external?

609. Timing: when do the effects of the communication take place?

610. What is the stakeholders level of authority?

611. Which stakeholders can influence others?

612. What is Research And Development Tax Credit project communications management?

613. Why do you manage communications?

614. How were corresponding initiatives successful?

615. Do you ask; can you recommend others for you to talk with about this initiative?

616. What is the political influence?

617. How much time does it take to do it?

618. How will the person responsible for executing

the communication item be notified?

619. In your work, how much time is spent on stakeholder identification?

620. Are others needed?

621. Who will use or be affected by the result of a Research And Development Tax Credit project?

622. Why is stakeholder engagement important?

623. How do you manage communications?

624. Why manage stakeholders?

625. Are the stakeholders getting the information others need, are others consulted, are concerns addressed?

2.31 Risk Management Plan: Research And Development Tax Credit

626. Are staff committed for the duration of the product?

627. How would you suggest monitoring for risk transition indicators?

628. What other risks are created by choosing an avoidance strategy?

629. Which risks should get the attention?

630. Are there new risks that mitigation strategies might introduce?

631. Does the software engineering team have the right mix of skills?

632. Financial risk: can your organization afford to undertake the Research And Development Tax Credit project?

633. Technology risk: is the Research And Development Tax Credit project technically feasible?

634. Do you train all developers in the process?

635. Mitigation -how can you avoid the risk?

636. Can the risk be avoided by choosing a different alternative?

637. Is security a central objective?

638. Who has experience with this?

639. Where are you confronted with risks during the business phases?

640. Can it be changed quickly?

641. What is the probability the risk avoidance strategy will be successful?

642. Are Research And Development Tax Credit project requirements stable?

2.32 Risk Register: Research And Development Tax Credit

643. Is further information required before making a decision?

644. Are there any knock-on effects/impact on any of the other areas?

645. Assume the risk event or situation happens, what would the impact be?

646. Methodology: how will risk management be performed on this Research And Development Tax Credit project?

647. Can the likelihood and impact of failing to achieve corresponding recommendations and action plans be assessed?

648. What can be done about it?

649. What is the probability and impact of the risk occurring?

650. What is a Community Risk Register?

651. Who is accountable?

652. Do you require further engagement?

653. Who needs to know about this?

654. What further options might be available for responding to the risk?

655. Severity Prediction?

656. Having taken action, how did the responses effect change, and where is the Research And Development Tax Credit project now?

657. Preventative actions - planned actions to reduce the likelihood a risk will occur and/or reduce the seriousness should it occur. What should you do now?

658. What is your current and future risk profile?

659. What is the reason for current performance gaps and do the risks and opportunities identified previously account for this?

660. What are the major risks facing the Research And Development Tax Credit project?

661. Amongst the action plans and recommendations that you have to introduce are there some that could stop or delay the overall program?

662. How well are risks controlled?

2.33 Probability and Impact Assessment: Research And Development Tax Credit

663. Do benefits and chances of success outweigh potential damage if success is not attained?

664. Risk may be made during which step of risk management?

665. Has something like this been done before?

666. Risk categorization -which of your categories has more risk than others?

667. When and how will the recent breakthroughs in basic research lead to commercial products?

668. What should be the level of difficulty in handling the technology?

669. How are you working with risks?

670. What risks are necessary to achieve success?

671. What are the current requirements of the customer?

672. Which role do you have in the Research And Development Tax Credit project?

673. How do risks change during a Research And Development Tax Credit project life cycle?

674. Will there be an increase in the political conservatism?

675. What things are likely to change?

676. Do end-users have realistic expectations?

677. Are there any Research And Development Tax Credit projects similar to this one in existence?

678. How is the Research And Development Tax Credit project going to be managed?

679. Will new information become available during the Research And Development Tax Credit project?

680. What things might go wrong?

681. Do requirements put excessive performance constraints on the product?

682. Have top software and customer managers formally committed to support the Research And Development Tax Credit project?

2.34 Probability and Impact Matrix: Research And Development Tax Credit

683. Degree of confidence in estimated size estimate?

684. Does the Research And Development Tax Credit project team have experience with the technology to be implemented?

685. What will be the impact or consequence if the risk occurs?

686. Are the risk data complete?

687. Sensitivity analysis -which risks will have the most impact on the Research And Development Tax Credit project?

688. What is the likely future demand of the customer?

689. How would you assess the risk management process in the Research And Development Tax Credit project?

690. Lay ground work for future returns?

691. To what extent is the chosen technology maturing?

692. What would be the best solution?

693. How much is the probability of the risk

occurring?

694. What are the likely future requirements?

695. Does the customer have a solid idea of what is required?

696. What are the chances the risk events will occur?

697. What are the chances the event will occur?

698. What is the industrial relations prevailing in this organization?

699. How carefully have the potential competitors been identified?

700. Which of your Research And Development Tax Credit projects should be selected when compared with other Research And Development Tax Credit projects?

701. Who should be notified of the occurrence of each of the risk indicators?

2.35 Risk Data Sheet: Research And Development Tax Credit

702. How do you handle product safely?

703. What are you weak at and therefore need to do better?

704. Whom do you serve (customers)?

705. Do effective diagnostic tests exist?

706. What can happen?

707. How can it happen?

708. What if client refuses?

709. What do you know?

710. Risk of what?

711. What do people affected think about the need for, and practicality of preventive measures?

712. What actions can be taken to eliminate or remove risk?

713. Type of risk identified?

714. Is the data sufficiently specified in terms of the type of failure being analyzed, and its frequency or probability?

715. How reliable is the data source?

716. Are new hazards created?

717. During work activities could hazards exist?

718. Will revised controls lead to tolerable risk levels?

719. Has a sensitivity analysis been carried out?

2.36 Procurement Management Plan: Research And Development Tax Credit

720. Are decisions captured in a decisions log?

721. Has the budget been baselined?

722. Has a sponsor been identified?

723. Are schedule deliverables actually delivered?

724. Have Research And Development Tax Credit project team accountabilities & responsibilities been clearly defined?

725. Are key risk mitigation strategies added to the Research And Development Tax Credit project schedule?

726. Are meeting minutes captured and sent out after meetings?

727. Is it possible to track all classes of Research And Development Tax Credit project work (e.g. scheduled, un-scheduled, defect repair, etc.)?

728. Have the procedures for identifying budget variances been followed?

729. Are post milestone Research And Development Tax Credit project reviews (PMPR) conducted with your organization at least once a year?

730. Public engagement – did you get it right?

731. Do Research And Development Tax Credit project teams & team members report on status / activities / progress?

732. Are written status reports provided on a designated frequent basis?

733. Are the budget estimates reasonable?

734. Has the scope management document been updated and distributed to help prevent scope creep?

735. What are things that you need to improve?

736. In which phase of the Acquisition Process Cycle does source qualifications reside?

2.37 Source Selection Criteria: Research And Development Tax Credit

737. Is there collaboration among your evaluators?

738. Who must be notified?

739. When and what information can be considered with offerors regarding past performance?

740. How long will it take for the purchase cost to be the same as the lease cost?

741. What should be the contracting officers strategy?

742. What should preproposal conferences accomplish?

743. What source selection software is your team using?

744. What documentation should be used to support the selection decision?

745. Can you identify proposed teaming partners and/or subcontractors and consider the nature and extent of proposed involvement in satisfying the Research And Development Tax Credit project requirements?

746. What risks were identified in the proposals?

747. How should oral presentations be prepared for?

748. In order of importance, which evaluation criteria are the most critical to the determination of your overall rating?

749. How do you facilitate evaluation against published criteria?

750. How much weight should be placed on past performance information?

751. Is the contracting office likely to receive more purchase requests for this item or service during the coming year?

752. How should oral presentations be evaluated?

753. What documentation is necessary regarding electronic communications?

754. What past performance information should be requested?

755. What are the guiding principles for developing an evaluation report?

756. How is past performance evaluated?

2.38 Stakeholder Management Plan: Research And Development Tax Credit

757. Why would a customer be interested in a particular product or service?

758. Is stakeholder involvement adequate?

759. When would you develop a Research And Development Tax Credit project Business Plan?

760. Has the Research And Development Tax Credit project manager been identified?

761. Are you meeting your customers expectations consistently?

762. How many Research And Development Tax Credit project staff does this specific process affect?

763. Does the Research And Development Tax Credit project have a Quality Culture?

764. Which impacts could serve as impediments?

765. What guidelines or procedures currently exist that must be adhered to (eg departmental accounting procedures)?

766. Has the business need been clearly defined?

767. Have Research And Development Tax Credit project management standards and procedures been

established and documented?

768. After observing execution of process, is it in compliance with the documented Plan?

769. Are tasks tracked by hours?

770. Has a structured approach been used to break work effort into manageable components (WBS)?

771. Who is accountable for the achievement of the targeted outcome(s) and reports on the progress towards the target?

772. Do Research And Development Tax Credit project managers participating in the Research And Development Tax Credit project know the Research And Development Tax Credit projects true status first hand?

773. Who is responsible for accepting the reports produced by the process?

2.39 Change Management Plan: Research And Development Tax Credit

774. Is there an adequate supply of people for the new roles?

775. When developing your communication plan do you address : When should the given message be communicated?

776. Do you need new systems?

777. What new competencies will be required for the roles?

778. What method and medium would you use to announce a message?

779. Has the relevant business unit been notified of installation and support requirements?

780. How much change management is needed?

781. What did the people around you say about it?

782. What do you expect the target audience to do, say, think or feel as a result of this communication?

783. Are there resource implications for your communications strategy?

784. Do you need a new organizational structure?

785. Impact of systems implementation on organization change?

786. What are you trying to achieve as a result of communication?

787. What communication network would you use – informal or formal?

788. Who might be able to help you the most?

789. Change invariability confront many relationships especially the already stated that require a set of behaviours What roles with in your organization are affected and how?

790. What roles within your organization are affected, and how?

791. What tasks are needed?

792. Have the systems been configured and tested?

3.0 Executing Process Group: Research And Development Tax Credit

793. What is in place for ensuring adequate change control on Research And Development Tax Credit projects that involve outside contracts?

794. What is the product of your Research And Development Tax Credit project?

795. How do you enter durations, link tasks, and view critical path information?

796. What is involved in the solicitation process?

797. What type of information goes in the quality assurance plan?

798. Do the partners have sufficient financial capacity to keep up the benefits produced by the programme?

799. Who will provide training?

800. Are escalated issues resolved promptly?

801. When will the Research And Development Tax Credit project be done?

802. What are the critical steps involved in selecting measures and initiatives?

803. How does a Research And Development Tax Credit project life cycle differ from a product life

cycle?

804. What are the main types of goods and services being outsourced?

805. Who will be the main sponsor?

806. Is the program supported by national and/or local organizations?

807. Does the Research And Development Tax Credit project team have enough people to execute the Research And Development Tax Credit project plan?

808. How is Research And Development Tax Credit project performance information created and distributed?

809. How well defined and documented were the Research And Development Tax Credit project management processes you chose to use?

810. Is the Research And Development Tax Credit project performing better or worse than planned?

3.1 Team Member Status Report: Research And Development Tax Credit

811. How will resource planning be done?

812. Will the staff do training or is that done by a third party?

813. Is there evidence that staff is taking a more professional approach toward management of your organizations Research And Development Tax Credit projects?

814. Does every department have to have a Research And Development Tax Credit project Manager on staff?

815. How it is to be done?

816. Does your organization have the means (staff, money, contract, etc.) to produce or to acquire the product, good, or service?

817. How much risk is involved?

818. Why is it to be done?

819. How can you make it practical?

820. The problem with Reward & Recognition Programs is that the truly deserving people all too often get left out. How can you make it practical?

821. What specific interest groups do you have in place?

822. How does this product, good, or service meet the needs of the Research And Development Tax Credit project and your organization as a whole?

823. Does the product, good, or service already exist within your organization?

824. Do you have an Enterprise Research And Development Tax Credit project Management Office (EPMO)?

825. Are your organizations Research And Development Tax Credit projects more successful over time?

826. When a teams productivity and success depend on collaboration and the efficient flow of information, what generally fails them?

827. Are the attitudes of staff regarding Research And Development Tax Credit project work improving?

828. What is to be done?

829. Are the products of your organizations Research And Development Tax Credit projects meeting customers objectives?

3.2 Change Request: Research And Development Tax Credit

830. Describe how modifications, enhancements, defects and/or deficiencies shall be notified (e.g. Problem Reports, Change Requests etc) and managed. Detail warranty and/or maintenance periods?

831. Should staff call into the helpdesk or go to the website?

832. What needs to be communicated?

833. Screen shots or attachments included in a Change Request?

834. Are there requirements attributes that are strongly related to the complexity and size?

835. Why do you want to have a change control system?

836. How is quality being addressed on the Research And Development Tax Credit project?

837. How well do experienced software developers predict software change?

838. Who can suggest changes?

839. When do you create a change request?

840. How are changes requested (forms, method of communication)?

841. Who needs to approve change requests?

842. Have all related configuration items been properly updated?

843. Are there requirements attributes that can discriminate between high and low reliability?

844. What are the requirements for urgent changes?

845. What are the basic mechanics of the Change Advisory Board (CAB)?

846. What kind of information about the change request needs to be captured?

847. What must be taken into consideration when introducing change control programs?

848. How many times must the change be modified or presented to the change control board before it is approved?

3.3 Change Log: Research And Development Tax Credit

849. Is the change request within Research And Development Tax Credit project scope?

850. Is the change backward compatible without limitations?

851. How does this relate to the standards developed for specific business processes?

852. Who initiated the change request?

853. Will the Research And Development Tax Credit project fail if the change request is not executed?

854. Do the described changes impact on the integrity or security of the system?

855. Where do changes come from?

856. How does this change affect the timeline of the schedule?

857. Is this a mandatory replacement?

858. Is the submitted change a new change or a modification of a previously approved change?

859. Does the suggested change request represent a desired enhancement to the products functionality?

860. When was the request approved?

861. How does this change affect scope?

862. When was the request submitted?

863. Is the requested change request a result of changes in other Research And Development Tax Credit project(s)?

864. Should a more thorough impact analysis be conducted?

865. Is the change request open, closed or pending?

3.4 Decision Log: Research And Development Tax Credit

866. Decision-making process; how will the team make decisions?

867. What is the average size of your matters in an applicable measurement?

868. Is everything working as expected?

869. What makes you different or better than others companies selling the same thing?

870. Is your opponent open to a non-traditional workflow, or will it likely challenge anything you do?

871. What is your overall strategy for quality control / quality assurance procedures?

872. What are the cost implications?

873. Do strategies and tactics aimed at less than full control reduce the costs of management or simply shift the cost burden?

874. How do you know when you are achieving it?

875. It becomes critical to track and periodically revisit both operational effectiveness; Are you noticing all that you need to, and are you interpreting what you see effectively?

876. Which variables make a critical difference?

877. How effective is maintaining the log at facilitating organizational learning?

878. Meeting purpose; why does this team meet?

879. At what point in time does loss become unacceptable?

880. How does the use a Decision Support System influence the strategies/tactics or costs?

881. Does anything need to be adjusted?

882. What was the rationale for the decision?

883. Behaviors; what are guidelines that the team has identified that will assist them with getting the most out of team meetings?

884. Linked to original objective?

885. Who is the decisionmaker?

3.5 Quality Audit: Research And Development Tax Credit

886. How does your organization know that its system for staff performance planning and review is appropriately effective and constructive?

887. Are there appropriate indicators for monitoring the effectiveness and efficiency of processes?

888. Why are you trying to do it?

889. How does your organization know that its systems for assisting staff with career planning and employment placements are appropriately effective and constructive?

890. How does your organization know that the quality of its supervisors is appropriately effective and constructive?

891. How does your organization know that its support services planning and management systems are appropriately effective and constructive?

892. How does your organization know that the support for its staff is appropriately effective and constructive?

893. How does your organization know that its processes for managing severance are appropriately effective, constructive and fair?

894. How do you indicate the extent to which your personnel would be expected to contribute to the work effort?

895. Statements of intent remain exactly that until they are put into effect. The next step is to deploy the already stated intentions. In other words, do the plans happen in reality?

896. For each device to be reconditioned, are device specifications, such as appropriate engineering drawings, component specifications and software specifications, maintained?

897. What experience do staff have in the type of work that the audit entails?

898. How does your organization know that its Governance system is appropriately effective and constructive?

899. How does your organization know that its promotions system is appropriately effective, constructive and fair?

900. What review processes are in place for your organizations major activities?

901. How does your organization know that its systems for communicating with and among staff are appropriately effective and constructive?

902. Are the intentions consistent with external obligations (such as applicable laws)?

903. Is the continuing professional education of key

personnel account fored in detail?

904. Are people allowed to contribute ideas?

905. If your organization thinks it is doing something well, can it prove this?

3.6 Team Directory: Research And Development Tax Credit

906. Where should the information be distributed?

907. Process decisions: which organizational elements and which individuals will be assigned management functions?

908. Where will the product be used and/or delivered or built when appropriate?

909. Is construction on schedule?

910. Days from the time the issue is identified?

911. Who should receive information (all stakeholders)?

912. When will you produce deliverables?

913. How will the team handle changes?

914. What are you going to deliver or accomplish?

915. Who will report Research And Development Tax Credit project status to all stakeholders?

916. Who will talk to the customer?

917. Decisions: is the most suitable form of contract being used?

918. Process decisions: are contractors adequately prosecuting the work?

919. Why is the work necessary?

920. Who will be the stakeholders on your next Research And Development Tax Credit project?

921. Process decisions: are all start-up, turn over and close out requirements of the contract satisfied?

922. How does the team resolve conflicts and ensure tasks are completed?

923. Timing: when do the effects of communication take place?

3.7 Team Operating Agreement: Research And Development Tax Credit

924. What administrative supports will be put in place to support the team and the teams supervisor?

925. What types of accommodations will be formulated and put in place for sustaining the team?

926. Are there more than two native languages represented by your team?

927. Do you determine the meeting length and time of day?

928. What is teaming?

929. Do you use a parking lot for any items that are important and outside of the agenda?

930. Has the appropriate access to relevant data and analysis capability been granted?

931. Is compensation based on team and individual performance?

932. Reimbursements: how will the team members be reimbursed for expenses and time commitments?

933. What are the safety issues/risks that need to be addressed and/or that the team needs to consider?

934. Did you recap the meeting purpose, time, and

expectations?

935. What individual strengths does each team member bring to the group?

936. Confidentiality: how will confidential information be handled?

937. Are team roles clearly defined and accepted?

938. What is culture?

939. What are the boundaries (organizational or geographic) within which you operate?

940. Are there the right people on your team?

941. What is the anticipated procedure (recruitment, solicitation of volunteers, or assignment) for selecting team members?

942. Are there differences in access to communication and collaboration technology based on team member location?

3.8 Team Performance Assessment: Research And Development Tax Credit

943. To what degree is there a sense that only the team can succeed?

944. To what degree can the team ensure that all members are individually and jointly accountable for the teams purpose, goals, approach, and work-products?

945. To what degree is the team cognizant of small wins to be celebrated along the way?

946. To what degree are fresh input and perspectives systematically caught and added (for example, through information and analysis, new members, and senior sponsors)?

947. To what degree does the team possess adequate membership to achieve its ends?

948. To what degree do team members understand one anothers roles and skills?

949. To what degree can the team measure progress against specific goals?

950. To what degree does the teams work approach provide opportunity for members to engage in open interaction?

951. To what degree do team members articulate the

teams work approach?

952. To what degree can all members engage in open and interactive considerations?

953. If you have criticized someones work for method variance in your role as reviewer, what was the circumstance?

954. To what degree does the teams approach to its work allow for modification and improvement over time?

955. To what degree are staff involved as partners in the improvement process?

956. To what degree do team members frequently explore the teams purpose and its implications?

957. How does Research And Development Tax Credit project termination impact Research And Development Tax Credit project team members?

958. To what degree can team members meet frequently enough to accomplish the teams ends?

959. To what degree are the goals realistic?

960. What makes opportunities more or less obvious?

961. When does the medium matter?

3.9 Team Member Performance Assessment: Research And Development Tax Credit

962. How do you currently use the time that is available?

963. How is assessment information achieved, stored?

964. Can your organization rate by exception and assume that most employees are performing at an acceptable level?

965. To what extent are systems and applications (e.g., game engine, mobile device platform) utilized?

966. How do you create a self-sustaining capacity for a collaborative culture?

967. What stakeholders must be involved in the development and oversight of the performance plan?

968. Do the goals support your organizations goals?

969. What happens if a team member disagrees with the Job Expectations?

970. How does your team work together?

971. What are best practices in use for the performance measurement system?

972. What are the basic principles and objectives of

performance measurement and assessment?

973. What qualities does a successful Team leader possess?

974. How was the determination made for which training platforms would be used (i.e., media selection)?

975. Is there reluctance to join a team?

976. Verify business objectives. Are they appropriate, and well-articulated?

977. How will they be formed?

978. What innovations (if any) are developed to realize goals?

3.10 Issue Log: Research And Development Tax Credit

979. What date was the issue resolved?

980. Who were proponents/opponents?

981. Are stakeholder roles recognized by your organization?

982. Who reported the issue?

983. Where do team members get information?

984. How often do you engage with stakeholders?

985. Persistence; will users learn a work around or will they be bothered every time?

986. What would have to change?

987. Who are the members of the governing body?

988. Is access to the Issue Log controlled?

989. What is the impact on the Business Case?

990. Do you feel more overwhelmed by stakeholders?

991. Are there potential barriers between the team and the stakeholder?

992. What does the stakeholder need from the team?

993. Why do you manage human resources?

994. Who is involved as you identify stakeholders?

995. Who is the issue assigned to?

996. Do you often overlook a key stakeholder or stakeholder group?

4.0 Monitoring and Controlling Process Group: Research And Development Tax Credit

997. Is progress on outcomes due to your program?

998. Based on your Research And Development Tax Credit project communication management plan, what worked well?

999. How can you monitor progress?

1000. Is there undesirable impact on staff or resources?

1001. How well did the team follow the chosen processes?

1002. Just how important is your work to the overall success of the Research And Development Tax Credit project?

1003. How well did the chosen processes fit the needs of the Research And Development Tax Credit project?

1004. Who needs to be involved in the planning?

1005. What is the timeline?

1006. What departments are involved in its daily operation?

1007. User: who wants the information and what are

they interested in?

1008. Measurable - are the targets measurable?

1009. Do clients benefit (change) from the services?

1010. How well did the chosen processes produce the expected results?

1011. How is Agile Research And Development Tax Credit project Management done?

1012. Did it work?

1013. What resources (both financial and non-financial) are available/needed?

1014. Where is the Risk in the Research And Development Tax Credit project?

1015. What good practices or successful experiences or transferable examples have been identified?

1016. Did you implement the program as designed?

4.1 Project Performance Report: Research And Development Tax Credit

1017. To what degree will the approach capitalize on and enhance the skills of all team members in a manner that takes into consideration other demands on members of the team?

1018. To what degree does the teams work approach provide opportunity for members to engage in results-based evaluation?

1019. To what degree are sub-teams possible or necessary?

1020. What is the degree to which rules govern information exchange between individuals within your organization?

1021. To what degree does the teams purpose constitute a broader, deeper aspiration than just accomplishing short-term goals?

1022. To what degree does the teams work approach provide opportunity for members to engage in fact-based problem solving?

1023. To what degree will team members, individually and collectively, commit time to help themselves and others learn and develop skills?

1024. To what degree are the demands of the task compatible with and converge with the mission and functions of the formal organization?

1025. To what degree is the information network consistent with the structure of the formal organization?

1026. To what degree are the tasks requirements reflected in the flow and storage of information?

1027. To what degree are the structures of the formal organization consistent with the behaviors in the informal organization?

1028. To what degree are the teams goals and objectives clear, simple, and measurable?

1029. To what degree do the structures of the formal organization motivate taskrelevant behavior and facilitate task completion?

1030. What is the PRS?

1031. To what degree can the cognitive capacity of individuals accommodate the flow of information?

1032. How will procurement be coordinated with other Research And Development Tax Credit project aspects, such as scheduling and performance reporting?

4.2 Variance Analysis: Research And Development Tax Credit

1033. Is the anticipated (firm and potential) business base Research And Development Tax Credit projected in a rational, consistent manner?

1034. Why do variances exist?

1035. Are work packages assigned to performing organizations?

1036. What does an unfavorable overhead volume variance mean?

1037. Are indirect costs charged to the appropriate indirect pools and incurring organization?

1038. Are overhead cost budgets established for each department which has authority to incur overhead costs?

1039. Does the contractors system provide unit or lot costs when applicable?

1040. Do work packages consist of discrete tasks which are adequately described?

1041. At what point should variances be isolated and brought to the attention of the management?

1042. Who are responsible for the establishment of budgets and assignment of resources for overhead performance?

1043. What does a favorable labor efficiency variance mean?

1044. What is the expected future profitability of each customer?

1045. Are data elements reconcilable between internal summary reports and reports forwarded to the stakeholders?

1046. Is the market likely to continue to grow at this rate next year?

1047. Does the contractors system identify work accomplishment against the schedule plan?

1048. Other relevant issues of Variance Analysis -selling price or gross margin?

1049. How have the setting and use of standards changed over time?

1050. Can the contractor substantiate work package and planning package budgets?

1051. Are there quarterly budgets with quarterly performance comparisons?

4.3 Earned Value Status: Research And Development Tax Credit

1052. If earned value management (EVM) is so good in determining the true status of a Research And Development Tax Credit project and Research And Development Tax Credit project its completion, why is it that hardly any one uses it in information systems related Research And Development Tax Credit projects?

1053. Where are your problem areas?

1054. Earned value can be used in almost any Research And Development Tax Credit project situation and in almost any Research And Development Tax Credit project environment. it may be used on large Research And Development Tax Credit projects, medium sized Research And Development Tax Credit projects, tiny Research And Development Tax Credit projects (in cut-down form), complex and simple Research And Development Tax Credit projects and in any market sector. some people, of course, know all about earned value, they have used it for years - but perhaps not as effectively as they could have?

1055. How does this compare with other Research And Development Tax Credit projects?

1056. Verification is a process of ensuring that the developed system satisfies the stakeholders agreements and specifications; Are you building the product right? What do you verify?

1057. Validation is a process of ensuring that the developed system will actually achieve the stakeholders desired outcomes; Are you building the right product? What do you validate?

1058. Where is evidence-based earned value in your organization reported?

1059. How much is it going to cost by the finish?

1060. What is the unit of forecast value?

1061. Are you hitting your Research And Development Tax Credit projects targets?

1062. When is it going to finish?

4.4 Risk Audit: Research And Development Tax Credit

1063. Should additional substantive testing be conducted because of the risk audit results?

1064. Who is responsible for what?

1065. Do you have a consistent repeatable process that is actually used?

1066. How can the strategy fail/achieved?

1067. Does your organization have or has considered the need for insurance covers: public liability, professional indemnity and directors and officers liability?

1068. What are risks and how do you manage them?

1069. When your organization is entering into a major contract, does it seek legal advice?

1070. Are testing tools available and suitable?

1071. Do you have an emergency plan?

1072. Number of users of the product?

1073. Does your organization have a social media policy and procedure?

1074. Are Research And Development Tax Credit

project requirements stable?

1075. Where will the next scandal or adverse media involving your organization come from?

1076. Risks with Research And Development Tax Credit projects or new initiatives?

1077. How do you manage risk?

1078. What events or circumstances could affect the achievement of your objectives?

1079. What can you do to manage outcomes?

1080. Are requirements fully understood by the team and customers?

1081. Does the adoption of a business risk audit approach change internal control documentation and testing practices?

1082. How risk averse are you?

4.5 Contractor Status Report: Research And Development Tax Credit

1083. Are there contractual transfer concerns?

1084. How is risk transferred?

1085. What process manages the contracts?

1086. What are the minimum and optimal bandwidth requirements for the proposed solution?

1087. Describe how often regular updates are made to the proposed solution. Are corresponding regular updates included in the standard maintenance plan?

1088. What is the average response time for answering a support call?

1089. If applicable; describe your standard schedule for new software version releases. Are new software version releases included in the standard maintenance plan?

1090. What was the overall budget or estimated cost?

1091. How does the proposed individual meet each requirement?

1092. What was the actual budget or estimated cost for your organizations services?

1093. How long have you been using the services?

1094. What was the final actual cost?

1095. What was the budget or estimated cost for your organizations services?

1096. Who can list a Research And Development Tax Credit project as organization experience, your organization or a previous employee of your organization?

4.6 Formal Acceptance: Research And Development Tax Credit

1097. What is the Acceptance Management Process?

1098. Does it do what Research And Development Tax Credit project team said it would?

1099. How does your team plan to obtain formal acceptance on your Research And Development Tax Credit project?

1100. Is formal acceptance of the Research And Development Tax Credit project product documented and distributed?

1101. Was the Research And Development Tax Credit project managed well?

1102. What function(s) does it fill or meet?

1103. Do you buy pre-configured systems or build your own configuration?

1104. Have all comments been addressed?

1105. Who supplies data?

1106. Was business value realized?

1107. Was the sponsor/customer satisfied?

1108. What was done right?

1109. How well did the team follow the methodology?

1110. What are the requirements against which to test, Who will execute?

1111. Was the Research And Development Tax Credit project goal achieved?

1112. Did the Research And Development Tax Credit project achieve its MOV?

1113. What lessons were learned about your Research And Development Tax Credit project management methodology?

1114. What can you do better next time?

1115. Was the Research And Development Tax Credit project work done on time, within budget, and according to specification?

1116. General estimate of the costs and times to complete the Research And Development Tax Credit project?

5.0 Closing Process Group: Research And Development Tax Credit

1117. How will you know you did it?

1118. Did you do things well?

1119. What can you do better next time, and what specific actions can you take to improve?

1120. When will the Research And Development Tax Credit project be done?

1121. What were things that you did well, and could improve, and how?

1122. Who are the Research And Development Tax Credit project stakeholders?

1123. Did the Research And Development Tax Credit project management methodology work?

1124. Were escalated issues resolved promptly?

1125. Were risks identified and mitigated?

1126. What will you do?

1127. Is the Research And Development Tax Credit project funded?

1128. Is this a follow-on to a previous Research And Development Tax Credit project?

1129. Were the outcomes different from the already stated planned?

1130. What areas were overlooked on this Research And Development Tax Credit project?

1131. If action is called for, what form should it take?

1132. Are there funding or time constraints?

1133. Were cost budgets met?

5.1 Procurement Audit: Research And Development Tax Credit

1134. Is the purchasing department organizationally independent of the departments using that function?

1135. Do the internal control systems function appropriate?

1136. Where required, were candidates registered as approved contractors, suppliers or service providers or certified by relevant bodies?

1137. Are there internal control systems in place to secure that laws and regulations are observed?

1138. Where funding is being arranged by borrowings, do corresponding have the necessary approval and legal authority?

1139. Who are the key suppliers?

1140. Are all purchase orders signed by the purchasing agent?

1141. Are all pre-numbered checks accounted for on a regular basis?

1142. Were additional works strictly necessary for the completion of performance under the contract?

1143. When negotiation took place in successive stages, was this practice stated in the procurement documents and was it done in accordance with the award criteria stated?

1144. Are all complaints of late or incorrect payment sent to a person independent of the already stated having cash disbursement responsibilities?

1145. Is the procurement function/unit organized the most appropriate way taking into consideration the actual tasks which the department has to carry out?

1146. Have the funding arrangements been agreed where payments take place over several financial periods?

1147. Have guidelines been set up for how the procurement process should be conducted?

1148. Is trend analysis performed on expenditures made by key employees and by vendor?

1149. Is the procurement process fully digitalized?

1150. Proper and complete records of transactions and events are maintained?

1151. Is the minutes book kept current?

1152. Does the procurement function/unit have the ability to negotiate with customers and suppliers?

1153. If a purchase order calls for a cost-plus agreement, is the method of determining how final charges will be determined specified?

5.2 Contract Close-Out: Research And Development Tax Credit

1154. Have all acceptance criteria been met prior to final payment to contractors?

1155. Have all contract records been included in the Research And Development Tax Credit project archives?

1156. Are the signers the authorized officials?

1157. Change in knowledge?

1158. Change in circumstances?

1159. Change in attitude or behavior?

1160. What happens to the recipient of services?

1161. Was the contract type appropriate?

1162. How/when used ?

1163. What is capture management?

1164. Has each contract been audited to verify acceptance and delivery?

1165. Parties: Authorized?

1166. Have all contracts been closed?

1167. Was the contract sufficiently clear so as not to result in numerous disputes and misunderstandings?

1168. Why Outsource?

1169. Was the contract complete without requiring numerous changes and revisions?

1170. How does it work?

1171. Have all contracts been completed?

1172. How is the contracting office notified of the automatic contract close-out?

1173. Parties: who is involved?

5.3 Project or Phase Close-Out: Research And Development Tax Credit

1174. Planned completion date?

1175. What could be done to improve the process?

1176. Is there a clear cause and effect between the activity and the lesson learned?

1177. Did the Research And Development Tax Credit project management methodology work?

1178. Does the lesson educate others to improve performance?

1179. In preparing the Lessons Learned report, should it reflect a consensus viewpoint, or should the report reflect the different individual viewpoints?

1180. What security considerations needed to be addressed during the procurement life cycle?

1181. What is the information level of detail required for each stakeholder?

1182. What hierarchical authority does the stakeholder have in your organization?

1183. What advantages do the an individual interview have over a group meeting, and vice-versa?

1184. Is the lesson based on actual Research And

Development Tax Credit project experience rather than on independent research?

1185. What were the actual outcomes?

1186. What is a Risk?

1187. What is in it for you?

1188. Complete yes or no?

1189. Who controlled the resources for the Research And Development Tax Credit project?

1190. Have business partners been involved extensively, and what data was required for them?

5.4 Lessons Learned: Research And Development Tax Credit

1191. Did the Research And Development Tax Credit project improve the team members reputations, skills, personal development?

1192. Was sufficient advance training conducted and/or information provided to enable the already stated affected by the changes to adjust to and accommodate them?

1193. Would you spend your own time fixing this issue?

1194. What is the growth stage of the organization?

1195. Are you in full regulatory compliance?

1196. To what extent was the evolution of risks communicated?

1197. Are there any hidden conflicts of interest?

1198. What is the value of the deliverable?

1199. Recommendation: what do you recommend should be done to ensure that others throughout your organization can benefit from what you have learned?

1200. How effective were Research And Development Tax Credit project audits?

1201. How clear were you on your role in the Research And Development Tax Credit project?

1202. Was sufficient time allocated to review Research And Development Tax Credit project deliverables?

1203. How well was Research And Development Tax Credit project status communicated throughout your involvement in the Research And Development Tax Credit project?

1204. What on the Research And Development Tax Credit project worked well and was effective in the delivery of the product?

1205. How useful and complete was the Research And Development Tax Credit project document repository?

1206. What were the problems encountered in the Research And Development Tax Credit project-functional area relationship, why, and how could they be fixed?

1207. What are the internal fiscal constraints?

1208. What is the skill mix defined for the staffing?

1209. What is the impact of tax policy?

1210. How useful was the format and content of the Research And Development Tax Credit project Status Report to you?

Index

management 1, 3-6, 9-10, 17, 20, 28-30, 53, 73, 122, 134, 136, 138, 140, 142, 148-151, 154, 157, 161, 172, 174-176, 178, 184, 186, 192, 194, 196-198, 200, 202, 204, 206, 210-211, 214, 216, 219-221, 226, 228, 231, 241-242, 245, 247, 253-255, 259, 261

manager   8, 10, 33-34, 214, 220
managers   2, 128, 171, 205, 215
manages   251
managing   2, 128, 133-134, 172, 228
mandate   132
mandatory   224
manner   19, 75, 154-155, 157, 192-193, 243, 245
mapped   35
margin 157, 246
marked   149
market 16, 41, 73, 94, 98, 110, 132, 246-247
marketer   8
marketing   151
Master 155, 175
material   155, 193
materials   1, 149
matrices   146
Matrix 3, 5, 134, 146, 192, 206
matter 31, 71-72, 97, 104, 107, 236
matters   226
mature 192
maturing   206
maximize   93
maximizing   125
maximum   129
meaningful   40, 103
measurable   25, 29, 154, 242, 244
measure   2, 10, 22, 30, 32, 37-38, 40-41, 44, 47, 52, 64, 69, 75, 79, 131, 135, 182, 185, 187-188, 190, 235
measured   17, 39, 41, 46, 80, 188
measures   38-41, 44, 52-53, 70, 86, 158, 189, 208, 218
measuring   86, 193
mechanical   1, 53
mechanics   223
mechanism   127, 151
mechanisms   134, 191
medium   216, 236, 247
meeting   27, 83, 88, 110, 149, 186, 194, 210, 214, 221, 227, 233, 261

purchasing   102, 257
purpose   2, 10, 21, 90, 92, 126, 132, 148, 170, 183, 227, 233,
235-236, 243
purposes   93, 95, 121
pursue 100
pursuing   117
qualified   29, 50-52, 55, 57, 60-62, 139
qualifies   50, 53, 56-57, 60-62
qualify 44, 47, 50, 53-57, 59-63
Qualifying   55
qualities   18, 238
quality 1, 4-6, 10, 38, 44-45, 51, 63, 86, 129, 137, 140-141, 158,
175, 178, 186, 188-191, 195-197, 214, 218, 222, 226, 228
quantified   39
quantify   37
quarterly   102, 246
question   11-12, 16, 24, 37, 49, 64, 78, 88, 135
questions   8-9, 11, 57, 143
quickly 10, 108, 201
raised 157
raising 137
rather 262
rating 213
rational   192, 245
rationale   110, 227
reached   17
readiness   101
readings   82
realistic   16, 106, 139, 205, 236
reality 229
realize 238
realized   107, 253
really   8, 97
reason 203
reasonable   181, 211
reasons   29, 124
reassess   140, 158
re-assign   161
reassigned   185
recast 181
receipt 59
receive   9-10, 33, 42, 94, 105, 113, 121, 213, 231
received   26, 107

CPSIA information can be obtained
at www.ICGtesting.com
Printed in the USA
BVHW041658120919

558313BV00013B/186/P